america's western edge

by john m. thompson

photographs by phil schermeister

NATIONAL GEOGRAPHIC

WASHINGTON, D.C.

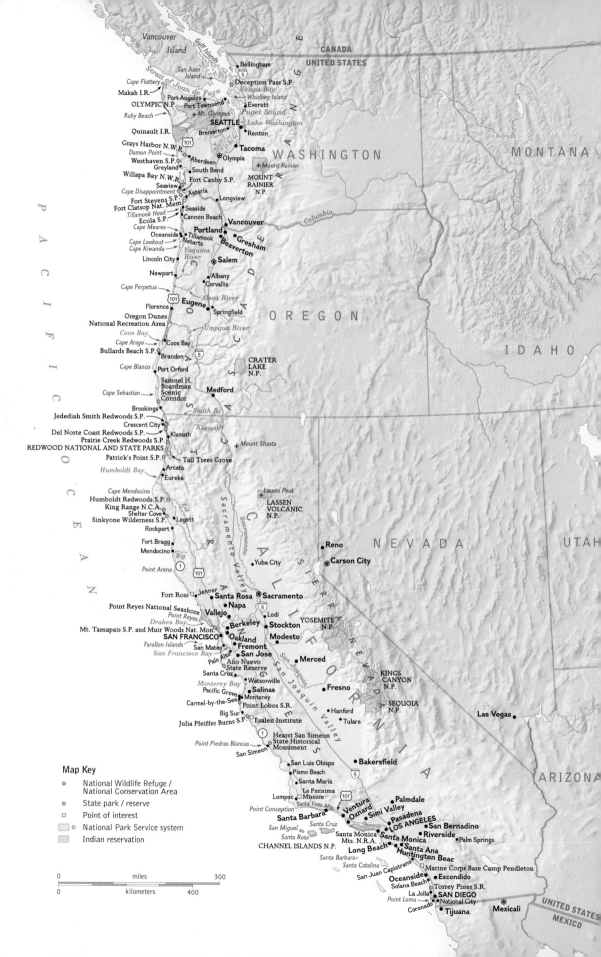

Page 1: A surfer at Oregon's Ecola State Park has an arched rock for a backdrop.
Pages 2-3: Sunset paints a mysterious mood along the Oregon coast.

introduction

✳

IN THE 1,300 MILES between San Diego and Seattle, the American dream lives on. It has been 150 years since the great westward migration, yet the possibilities here still seem as endless as the Pacific. People keep coming to the edge of the continent to lose themselves and find themselves, if only for a week or two. The liberal embrace of America's left bank is far-reaching—it takes in tree sitters and tree cutters, oyster farmers and movie stars, surfing bums and software tycoons, café artists and upstartists, Mexicans and Asians, Native Americans and more. The landscape also unspools in endless variations. From the population centers of southern California to the redwood forests farther north, from the wave-pounded cliffs of Oregon to the foggy islands of Puget Sound, the Pacific Coast delivers a variety show of stunning scenes.

With photographer Phil Schermeister's discerning eye for a guide, this book takes readers on a tour of the coast, from bottom to top, pausing in cities and seaside hamlets, state parks and wildlife refuges. In the first chapter we take a look at sunny Southern California and its teeming mix of lifestyles. Surfing culture, Spanish-influenced architecture, celebrity glitz, and scenes of breathtaking beauty all have their place here. Cabrillo National Monument, Channel Islands National Park, and Hearst Castle are but a few of the places we'll visit. The second chapter explores the northern California coast, from San Francisco and its bustling

The tide pools of Point Lobos State Reserve near Carmel reveal a rich stew of marine life.
The patterns, colors, and textures of these rocky coves play infinite variations on a coastal theme.

waterfront to the tall trees of Redwood National and State Parks. Along this rugged shore a white-knuckle highway follows the undulating coastal bluffs, crossing canyon bridges and touching down in secluded little beach-rimmed coves. In remnant virgin forests, just east of the highway, the world's tallest trees reach into the clouds.

Chapter Three investigates the Oregon Coast, where one state park after another has helped preserve the finest features of the shoreline. Lonely lighthouses and weathered trees perch atop steep headlands, wind-driven swells slam against sea stacks with a heart-pounding spray, and thousands of gray whales migrate through in winter and spring. The cliffs make perfect bleachers for watching the spectacles of nature, including the approach of storms from far out at sea. In the final chapter the subject is Washington's diverse coast, from the wide beaches in the south to the rain forests of Olympic National Park and the busy piers of Seattle. Out on the timeless San Juan Islands, life slows to the pace of a kayak paddle and a heron's flight. Fishermen cast their luck with the sea, as they have for thousands of years in these parts, and, as always, the sea obliges.

If the West Coast is filled with variety, what ties it together, making it distinct from every other region in the country? For one thing, it rains a lot in winter, especially in the north, where some spots routinely receive more than 100 inches of precipitation. But summers are blessed with good weather. What sailor Richard Henry Dana wrote about California in 1859 still applies to pretty much the whole coast: "In summer there can be no bad weather in California. Every day is pleasant. Nature forbids a drop of rain to fall by day or night, or a wind to excite itself beyond a fresh summer breeze."

Year-round the entire coast has moderate temperatures. Summers east of the Coast Ranges can be brutally hot and dry, while cool breezes fan the shore; in winter, it might be snowing inland, but on the shore the thermometer rarely dips below 40 degrees. The resulting coastal forest is a lush garden of spruce and cedar, ferns and mosses. As for landscape, the West Coast is routinely more dramatic than the East Coast. Instead of a long lazy sweep of low coastal plain ending in a gentle beach, the West Coast suddenly plunges from the mountains to the sea, where waves gouge out precipitous cliffs and huge rocks stand like islands in the surf.

All along the coast, wildlife is abundant. Noisy sea lions and seals populate the coves and offshore rocks, as do seabirds by the hundreds of thousands. Puffins, murres, guillemots, and cormorants dive for fish, then fly back to their nests to share the catch of the hour. In tide pools up and down the Pacific Coast, sea stars

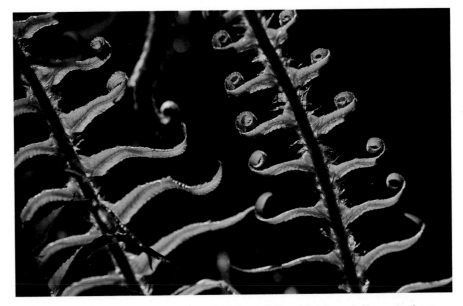

The multifaceted terrain of California's Point Reyes National Seashore shelters a wondrous collection of plant and animal species, including more than a dozen kinds of ferns.

cling to smooth stones, anemones sway with the waves, and a host of other marine life hides under rocks and in crevices, incessantly washed by the sea. Salmon and steelhead trout return from the sea to the rivers where they were born; they swim upstream, spawn, and die. And the cycle begins again.

One thing that sets this coast apart, literally, is plate tectonics. The Pacific Plate grinds northwest against the North American Plate. The continent is almost wholly contained on the latter plate, but not quite. A piece of it, extending from Southern California up nearly to Mendocino, lies on the Pacific Plate. Slippage along the dividing line, the San Andreas Fault, created the Coast Ranges and continues to shift the topography by imperceptible degrees—about an inch a year.

In the meantime, the shape of America's sunset coast can pose any number of playful conundrums. Is it a parenthesis, or a convex window on the world? A cutting edge, the prow of our ship to the future, or a rounded rump, the butt of our jokes? It's all of these and more. It was in the 1850s when Horace Greeley exhorted, "Go west, young man, and grow up with the country." Yet going west is still a rite of passage for people young and old. Here in this raw landscape, toes over the edge of the continent, you still feel on the verge of something new. From countless high bluffs the Pacific looks more vast than anything on Earth, as though the frontier only begins here. Somewhere out there in 6,000 miles of ocean the west ends and the east begins. The new world greets the old where the sun melts into the horizon. But right here at the fringe of the Pacific is our leaping-off place, the place where our journey begins and ends. ✸

sun-spangled shores

Amtrak's Coast Starlight hugs the coast near Santa Barbara.

SOUTHERN CALIFORNIA

❋

FROM SAN DIEGO TO SANTA CRUZ, youth is forever; the id triumphs; the creative impulse has no limits. Sunny Southern California is America's final frontier realized. Here in our dazzling paradise-on-a-fault-line dreams are made and illusions shattered, Hollywood deals go down with the ocean-bound sun, bikini babes flex for surfer dudes, and Mediterranean breezes waft over the good, the bad, the beautiful and damned alike. Just off the choked freeways, a semitropical light eternally pans the supple skin of the sea, pacifying tempers, converting graspers of the good life into sun-worshiping seekers of inner serenity.

At the southern end of America's Pacific coast, San Diego is blessed with an almost perfect climate—a year-round average temperature of 70 degrees, with scant rainfall that usually occurs in winter. Because of the ocean currents and breezes, summers are actually cooler here than in Los Angeles. With miles of blissful beaches along its 70-mile coastline, a long and attractive waterfront, Spanish Colonial-style mansions, and handsome parks landscaped with palms and flowers, this city of 1.2 million—seventh largest in the nation, second largest in California—deserves a reputation equal to Los Angeles, if not San Francisco. Less than 20 miles from the Mexican border, San Diego sports a multicultural mix that is more prevalent here than anywhere else in the state—neighborhoods, restaurants, radio stations, and signs attest to an ongoing Spanish influence.

All hands to the deck: Sturdy athletes prepare their shell for the San Diego Crew Classic.
The April competition in Mission Bay attracts more than 3,000 rowers from around the country.

The first European to arrive was Portuguese explorer Juan Rodriguez Cabrillo, who sailed into the harbor in the service of Spain in 1542. Sixty years later, a party of Spanish sailors gave the harbor and surrounding land the name San Diego, to honor a saint's feast day. But it was not until 1769 that anything in the way of a settlement was begun. In that year Padre Junipero Serra established California's first Spanish mission on Presidio Hill, overlooking what would become the city. The mission and military garrison hung on through Indian attacks and isolation, and after Mexican independence in 1821 the town began to grow. But slowly. Although the end of the Mexican-American War in 1848 meant that San Diego belonged to the United States, it was virtually overlooked during the gold rush that brought a flood of settlers to California. It took an outsider, a businessman from San Francisco, to see the potential of building up the waterfront area. The farsighted Alonzo Horton bought up property and promoted and sold it in his hometown, and on the "New Town" site the core of modern San Diego rose. By the 1870s there were buildings all over the waterfront, and outside of town were groves of oranges, pears, apples, figs, and olives.

The bombing of Pearl Harbor in 1941 propelled San Diego into the forefront of modern American life. It became home base of the U.S. Navy's Pacific fleet, which brought a huge influx of military and industrial workers, many of whom stayed on after the war. San Diego now holds the largest naval air station on the West Coast. The development of 4,600-acre Mission Bay Park in the 1960s turned a former swamp into a swank scene of nightclubs, beaches, man-made islands, and the popular Sea-World marine park. Since then skyscrapers and new homes have continued to rise, as San Diego plays host to big-time conventions, sports, entertainment, and tourism, and the conflict between development and conservation looms as large here as in any big city. But all in all this is a city in tune with its natural beauty and salubrious climate.

The best way to get an overview of San Diego, its coastal setting, and its history is to drive to the tip of Point Loma, which helps form the mouth of San Diego Bay. Out here on a 400-foot-high sandstone ridge covered with coastal sage scrub, Cabrillo National Monument pays tribute to the European discovery of the United States Pacific coast. Cabrillo and his crew left the first European footprints on California soil in September 1542. Shortly after departing, Cabrillo got into a scrape with some Indians on the Channel Islands, had a fall, and died of complications. The crew went on as far north as Oregon, then returned to Mexico, considering the expedition a bust. Yet the sensational view here of San Diego's skyline and bay shows that those early explorations were ultimately worth the trouble. Sailboats and commercial and naval ships steer through the harbor mouth. East of the city rise the gentle

Cuyamaca Mountains, while the view south sweeps across the sparkling bay and ocean to Mexico. The park's 1855 lighthouse ranks as one of the oldest on the West Coast. But at 422 feet above the sea, it was too high—coastal fog often rendered it useless. A new lighthouse was built in 1891 below the cloud ceiling, but the old one still stands as a historical monument.

Less than a mile out in the Pacific, gray whales make their annual winter migration to Baja California. Curiously, fewer whales pass Point Loma now than they did in the 1970s, even though the population has increased. The mid-January peak has dropped from about 40 whales per hour to 8. One possible cause is that the high number of whale-watching boats, some of which venture closer than the 100-yard minimum, has forced whales to avoid the area. Back on shore, other species have also run afoul of humans in recent decades. Abalones and owl limpets used to be plentiful in the area's rocky tide pools; now limpets are rare even in Cabrillo's protected waters, and abalones are nearly nonexistent. Both these shellfish are simply too tempting to human taste buds.

Between Point Loma and downtown San Diego, a curving peninsula holds the upscale community of Coronado, with its tony boutiques, restaurants, condos, and hotels, including the most famous hotel in the city. *(Continued on page 24)*

A comfortable mix of laissez-faire lifestyles pervades sunny La Jolla, where a day at the ocean might mean a formal wedding, or a shirts-off lie about, or both at the same time.

Its beacon days over, the Old Point Loma Lighthouse at San Diego's Cabrillo National Monument
now serves duty as a museum of 19th-century coastal life.

A street fair in Chicano Park celebrates San Diego's vibrant Mexican-American culture. One of every four San Diego County residents is Latino, the vast majority of Mexican origin.

Since opening in 1888, San Diego's Hotel Del Coronado has hosted a litany of the rich and famous, and served as the setting for many films, including the perennial favorite *Some Like It Hot*.

Bathed in evening and street light, the Mission San Luis Rey graces a hillside north of San Diego.
The sprawling "king of missions" was founded in 1798.

With a little help from a friend, a kayaker heads for the waves at **Torrey Pines State Reserve**, a park that includes rare trees, high bluffs, steep canyons, a tidal marsh, and a gravelly beach.

Youngsters test the waters at Huntington State Beach, a three-mile link in a chain of public beaches south of Los Angeles. California's surfing culture was born along here.

(*Continued from page 15*) The breathtaking Hotel del Coronado was built in 11 months in 1887-88, with Chinese workers laboring night and day. The ornate two-story grand lobby has greeted movie stars, kings, and commoners. From the playful red turrets to the fanciful chandeliers in the Oregon-pine dining room, it's easy to see why "The Del" reputedly served as a model for L. Frank Baum's Emerald City in *The Wizard of Oz*. Some people drop by just to take the historical tour, or have cocktails on the ocean-view terrace, or simply gape.

In Raymond Chandler's 1958 novel *Playback*, detective Philip Marlowe wryly describes a stretch of highway north of San Diego: "We went through a small shopping center, then the road widened and the houses on one side looked expensive and not new, while the houses on the other side looked very new and still not cheap." The description could apply to much of the San Diego suburbs today.

About 12 miles north of the city, the chic town of La Jolla is both a surfer's paradise and an enclave of the well-to-do. Local Indians called the area "la hoya" for its coastal grottoes; the Europeans adopted the place-name, which in Spanish (La Jolla) means "the jewel." The gems now are the multi-million-dollar Mediterranean villas peeking from lush gardens on the hills. On Prospect and adjoining streets, stylish restaurants, shops, and jazz clubs mix with well-maintained office buildings. As in most of Southern California, the tanned, open-collar look prevails in this relaxed haven of money and casual sophistication. Bikers, rollerbladers, and smartly dressed walkers parade along ocean-view walkways, while the beaches and coves around Point La Jolla stay packed with sunbathers, tide poolers, snorkelers, and sea lions.

La Jolla is perhaps best known for the Scripps Institution of Oceanography, just north of town. Founded in 1903 as the Marine Biological Association of San Diego in the Hotel del Coronado's boathouse, Scripps now is part of the University of California, boasting a 170-acre shoreline property. The illustrious institute and its four ships conduct ground-breaking research in oceanography, climatology, geophysics, geology, and biology. The superlative area beaches are not just objects of study—students and professors often take a break from classes on the back of a surfboard. A former graduate student told me, "One of the interesting things was that towels, surfboards, fishing poles, and bathing suits were always draped around the labs. Because where else would you store it? You didn't want some surfer running off with it. . . . We never used A/C, and I turned my heat on once in six years. That was because I'd been out swimming all day."

The Birch Aquarium at Scripps is one of the top aquariums on the West Coast (along with those in Monterey and Newport, Oregon). Its mission-style spread holds a state-of-the-art interactive museum, a demonstration tide pool, and more than 60 tanks, including a 13,000-gallon shark reef that attracts a steady stream of open-mouthed fans of the deep.

North of La Jolla, the curving coastline is dotted with tidy little beach towns whose sandy shores are packed throughout the long, almost endless summer with surfers, sunners, and volleyball players. Del Mar and Solana Beach keep a low, youthful profile away from the urban centers of SoCal; local news rarely gets more serious than a recent spate of dognappings, in which dogs left in locked cars were "found on the beach" and returned for $1,000 rewards.

Also along this stretch, the Torrey Pines State Reserve harbors one of the rarest tree species in the world. A few thousand gnarled Torrey pines grow here and on Santa Rosa Island off Santa Barbara, and nowhere else in the world. They dominate the park bluffs, overlooking the beach and ocean. From the beach one can behold surfers riding the swells, waiting for the right set; beyond them bottlenose dolphins roll like living waves. Hang gliders often launch from the cliffs above and either make beach landings or, with the right conditions and an experienced flier, land back on the cliff, saving a long return trek to the top.

North of the city of Oceanside, the Marine Corps' Camp Pendleton runs along the coast for nearly 20 miles and inland for 10 to 12 miles. This enormous spread ranks as one of the world's biggest amphibious training centers. It occupies land that belonged to a 19th-century land-grant rancho; the marines moved in during World War II. Since its value to the Marine Corps lies in its wildness, Camp Pendleton shelters coastal flora and fauna that might otherwise have disappeared under a bulldozer—the way much around Los Angeles already has.

✳

WHEN SEAMAN RICHARD HENRY DANA visited the mission at San Juan (just inland from current Dana Point) in 1835, he noted that "San Juan Bay is the only romantic spot on the coast. The country here for several miles is high table-land, running boldly to the shore and breaking off in a steep cliff, at the foot of which the waters of the Pacific are constantly dashing." This section of rocky shoreline, punctuated with pocket beaches, is still lightly populated. Nestled in the rolling foothills of the Santa Ana Mountains, the Mission San Juan Capistrano is as well known for the annual return of the swallows as for its architecture and history. From mid-March to mid-October they

Sailboats catch a glow in snug berths at Harbor Island, a 1.5-mile-long recreational peninsula made of 12 million cubic yards of mud and sand dredged from San Diego Bay in 1961.

congregate in the mission and town to nest, before the return flight to Argentina. They have been coming here since at least 1777, when they were noted in mission records. Artists began arriving in the early 1900s to capture the romantic mood of the adobe arcades, the gardens, and the ruins of the stone church, toppled in an 1812 earthquake.

The coast north to Los Angeles is strung with beach towns—Laguna Beach, Newport Beach, Huntington Beach, Long Beach—each larger than the one before. All but gone are the orange groves of Orange County, swallowed in spreading suburbs and highways. But the beaches, birthplace of the California surfing culture, are still wide and sandy, and open to all . . . assuming one is not deterred by rush-hour traffic weekdays and busy parking lots on weekends. Then there are the gated access points, mostly south of Newport Beach.

Offshore and onshore oil reserves turned these erstwhile seaside villages into tentacled boomtowns that have never stopped expanding. While smaller communities along here keep busy with light industry, yachting, and artistic endeavors, the port of Long Beach flexes its muscles as a major Pacific coast shipping center. Everything about Long Beach feels supersize—big harbor, big ships, big bridges, big buildings. Its major tourist attractions are huge: The *Queen Mary*, one of the largest passenger ships ever constructed, is moored at Long Beach Pier as a floating museum and hotel. And the capacious Aquarium of the Pacific opened in 1997 as one of the biggest on the West Coast. For the summer 2004 Olympic swimming trials, Long Beach put up a 10,000-seat temporary beachside swim stadium—about the size of the one used in Athens for the actual Olympics.

Just over 20 miles out in the ocean, Catalina (officially Santa Catalina) Island hearkens to an earlier, slower Southern California rhythm. With a couple of villages and few roads, this hilly island of delightful hidden coves and beaches lures boaters and day-trippers from the exhaust centers of greater Los Angeles. Indians, fur hunters, miners, and smugglers all took refuge here in the past. The resident buffalo herd began in 1924 with 14 animals used in the Hollywood film *The Vanishing American*; it now numbers in the hundreds. Chewing-gum tycoon William Wrigley, Jr., bought the island in 1919 and used it for years as the spring training venue for his Chicago Cubs baseball team. His heirs transferred nearly 90 percent of the land in 1975 to the Santa Catalina Island Conservancy to protect the island's natural beauty. Visitors now come to snorkel in the exceptionally clear waters, stroll past bungalows and restaurants, and take a look at Wrigley's Casino Building—not a gambling parlor, but a lavish 1920s Art Deco gathering place with a theater, ballroom, art gallery, and museum.

Motorists generally avoid the Palos Verdes Peninsula north of Long Beach. But a meander through here is the best approach to the beaches of Los Angeles. The lack of a freeway makes it a haven of expensive blufftop houses set on lush estates with expansive ocean views.

Raymond Chandler wrote that "in L.A. to be conspicuous you would have to drive a flesh-pink Mercedes-Benz with a sun porch on the roof and three pretty girls sunbathing." That was in the late 1950s. Now it might take more. On Venice Beach, for instance, weirdness is the rule. No one stands out among the pierced and tattooed, the vendors of crystals, the bikini-clad roller skaters, the dreadlocked sunglassed philosophers with their theories of life scrawled on cardboard boxes. Hordes of people, locals and tourists, throng the oceanfront walkway to buy ice cream and tacos, to take the sun, and, most of all, to see and be seen. The dazzling beach is almost too wide to bother crossing, hence relatively few people are actually out on the beach itself.

A friend of mine spent his teen years in Venice in the late 1970s, when it was evolving from a hippie hangout to a popular destination. "There were people there like 'Jimi Hendrix'—basically a homeless guy with wild hair who went around on skates playing guitar, until some rich guy took him in. Then he went around on skates in really nice clothes. There was also a nude part of the beach. *(Continued on page 32)*

San Diego's Pacific Beach is a veritable party scene of surfers waiting for just the right set.

A weight lifter sports his physique in an area of Venice known as the Pen, or Muscle Beach. The original Muscle Beach started in the 1920s up near Santa Monica Pier.

The larger than life is ordinary at Universal Studios Hollywood. The film studio here
no longer has tours, but rides in the theme park are like being inside a movie.

It was just becoming a tourist attraction then, and locals started playing up to tourists' perceptions—they fed off each other. And the joke about local traffic in L.A. was anywhere you wanted to go was always 20 minutes . . . depending on traffic. It's the same now except the prices. My wife's uncle just sold a house in downtown Santa Monica, a small house, for a million dollars. And the guy tore it down and built something else."

Just below Venice, the road ends at the channel to Marina del Rey's enormous yacht harbor. The town of Marina del Rey is a mix of honky-tonk cottages and fabulous canal-side houses with stucco walls, barrel-tile roofs, and lush gardens of azalea, crape myrtle, tulip trees, and hibiscus. The canals here and in Venice date back to 1904 when developers created a fantasy village, replete with bathhouses, bridges, and gondolas. Most of the canals were filled in and converted to roads for the ever more popular automobile.

In the middle of Venice Beach, the Muscle Beach area has migrated south from Santa Monica, where it started in the 1920s as a kind of gymnastics playground for kids, Hollywood stuntmen, and circus performers. Crowds of thousands would gather to watch impromptu feats of strength and dexterity. Since then, numerous stars and starlets and nameless hunks have worked out and shown off their fabulous muscles here, now-Governor Arnold Schwarzenegger among them. Local tourism bureaus are trying to promote the historical aspect over the bikini and beefcake exhibitionism, but the latter seems firmly entrenched for now.

To the north of Venice, the resort community of Santa Monica bristles with some of the state's smartest hotels. Glitterati entertain themselves in Mediterranean-style pools and leafy courtyards, or relax in sea-view suites before going out to meals prepared by world-famous chefs. Santa Monica's three-block Third Street Promenade is lined with shops and restaurants, fancy and plain. Crowds wander through all day and well into the night. Out on palm-shouldered Ocean Avenue, designer-clad joggers and bikers glide past homeless people whose shopping carts are laden with blankets and tattered belongings, while down in beach parking lots, skaters catch ocean breezes with big Dacron sails.

This medley of people is nowhere more evident than on the Santa Monica Pier. In addition to its eateries, bars, aquarium, roller coaster, and 1922 carousel, the pier is where Mexican fishermen drop lines and Asians sell T-shirts and sandals to Anglo visitors. Evoking amusement venues of an earlier era, this venerable institution is a postcard from 1912.

Around Santa Monica Bay, the sunny south-facing hills and beaches of Malibu are favored by Hollywood luminaries, whose houses hide among verdant gardens.

Instead of a town with a core and businesses, Malibu is really just an address. The rich and famous have to be somewhere—many of them choose to be here. A traveler on the Pacific Coast Highway will not see much of their lifestyle, but he will see the reason for their being here. For nearly 30 miles, the highway swings along the coast through the Santa Monica Mountains National Recreation Area. Not far out of Los Angeles, traffic is light—at least heading away from the city. Rugged canyons and ranches with old movie sets dapple the hills, which roll down to sandy beaches and bird-frequented lagoons.

FOR A PLACE WITH A REAL CENTER AND CHARACTER, one need not go far north. Santa Barbara is one of the most beautiful and livable cities on the West Coast. Set on a narrow terrace between the Pacific and the Santa Ynez Mountains, this town of red-tile roofs and whitewashed walls honors its Spanish colonial heritage. Santa Barbara was actually a jumble of architectural styles until the 1920s, when citizens decided to reclaim the town's roots. An earthquake in 1925 destroyed much of downtown, thus providing a tabula rasa for planners and designers to work from. The highlight of their efforts, the 1929 county courthouse is a veritable Moorish palace of imported tiles, hand-painted ceilings, graceful arches, and a sunken garden; the view from the 85-foot clock tower takes in the city and its hilly neighborhoods.

Another source of local pride, the Mission Santa Barbara is known as the "queen of missions" for its beauty. Still a parish church, the 1786 mission fits well in its foothill setting, with twin bell towers that look out upon the city. Trickling fountains and feathery linden trees grace the grounds; the worn stone floors and thick painted walls and beams inside attest to many years of service.

On a recent visit to Santa Barbara, I met up with a writer friend, and she took me down to Arroyo Burro Beach. We walked along a stretch known affectionately to surfers as "the pit." Hang gliders were preparing to launch from the green bluff above, while flocks of avocets skimmed the surf below. Out on the horizon you could see the hazy back of Santa Cruz Island and several oil platforms. In fact, afterward our shoes were caked with tarry sand from an old spill—a minor note in an otherwise uplifting interlude of sun and sea. My friend pointed out the Douglas Family Preserve. When a local preservation group needed money to purchase this property for parkland, actor Michael Douglas made a large donation and asked that the site *(Continued on page 40)*

A striking juxtaposition: At Nipomo Dunes, north of Santa Barbara, corduroy ridges of sand rise
and fall to a quiet beach. Yet also in the dunes, helmeted joyriders scream their beach buggies
within a fenced 1,500-acre recreation area.

A lowering sun burnishes cliffs of a wave-crashed cove near Monterey Bay.

Rough-edged beauty—Santa Cruz Island in Channel Islands National Park harbors tremendous
kelp forests and deep ocean trenches, home to a staggering variety of marine life.

Catching the morning sun, an old farm truck near Davenport advertises modern tastes. In addition
to strawberries, the bluff-top fields north of Santa Cruz are famous for brussels sprouts.

(Continued from page 33) be named in honor of his father, movie star Kirk Douglas. "Santa Barbara is so benignly beautiful and has such aggressively civic-minded citizens," my friend told me, "that the arts are really great here. And you have so many different sets of people—environmental, liberal types; Mexicans; homeless; artsy people; and, of course, millionaires. There's a no-growth policy, but we have ranchers in the north who want to split the county in half, because they don't like Santa Barbarans telling them what to do with their land."

After a game of tennis, we had lunch on her patio, surrounded by flowers and palms, the sparkling ocean in the distance, and, on the other side, green hills that turn tawny brown in the dry summers. Like many Santa Barbarans, my friend and her husband live in a modest-size house with a fabulous view. The price of real estate—median of nine hundred thousand for a house—keeps them content to stay where they are.

On clear days, Santa Cruz Island, less than 15 miles out, is visible from shore. Santa Cruz and its three island neighbors were a single landmass about 10,000 years ago, when the sea level was lower. Some 4,000 years later, as islands, they were inhabited by Chumash Indians, who paddled through rough currents to the mainland in driftwood canoes. Protected in 1938, they and tiny Santa Barbara Island to the south now make up Channel Islands National Park, home to an abundance of seals, sea lions, seabirds, and other animals. The islands' vast kelp forests harbor a tremendous variety of smaller marine life. Cut off from the mainland, the islands are rafts of biological uniqueness: The cat-size island fox lives only here, as do several species of plants. Getting to any one of the islands is an all-day proposition. The park service further controls access through a system of permits and, in some cases, by restricting trails to ranger-guided hikes only. But the lack of casual visitors is a bonus for wildlife.

Back on shore, the highway north of Santa Barbara passes through some of the cattle country my friends told me about, as well as huge fields of strawberries, interspersed with lovely meadows of waving grasses and wildflowers. Around the craggy coastline of Point Conception, the road stays inland. Richard Henry Dana describes the point from a 19th-century vantage: "Point Conception—the Cape Horn of California, where, the sailors say, it begins to blow the first of January, and blows until the last of December." A gale here "blowing like scissors and thumbscrews" ripped their mainsail head to foot.

Even several miles inland there's often a wind. At least there was when I visited La Purisma Mission outside Lompoc. The place is so deserted now it's hard to believe that as many as 800 people lived and worked here in the early 1800s. Breezes now waft through empty, high-ceilinged rooms, and the hills all around are unmarred by development. Huge stands of cactus grow beside the mission's adobe walls, and

The Neptune Pool looks just as it did in the halcyon days of Hearst Castle. Near the village of San Simeon, publisher William Randolph Hearst built his fabulous mansion from 1919 to 1947.

blue-flowering jacarandas frame a garden of herbs and fruit trees and spring-fed pools. The craftsmen, soldiers, Chumash, and Franciscan padres who lived in this gorgeous setting were self-sufficient—they grew their own vegetables, tended sheep, ground olives into oil, worked leather and iron. They worshiped in the tile-floored sanctuary, slept on narrow cots, and toiled in dim quarters. In 40 years the weaving room turned out some 40,000 blankets, for sale in Santa Barbara and for trade to passing ships. The restored mission bears the dusty smell of antiquity. With so much silence all about, one can imagine a time when the mission covered 300,000 acres. The current 1,900 acres are buffered by forest and agricultural lands as far as the eye can see, making this the most authentic setting of all the California missions.

NORTH OF SAN LUIS OBISPO the coast begins taking on a wildly rugged look. Banks of moist fog slide in from the ocean, then magically disappear, leaving views of waves crashing into fanged coves, and pleated hills rolling down to an engulfing sea. Sassy yellow mustard spices the hills, and calla lilies and poppies *(Continued on page 47)*

Bellicose elephant seal bulls compete for mates and space at Piedras Blancas, north of San Simeon. Other tough competitors, ice plants (left), or fig marigolds, add splashes of color to the coast, but at a price—the hardy exotics compete with native vegetation.

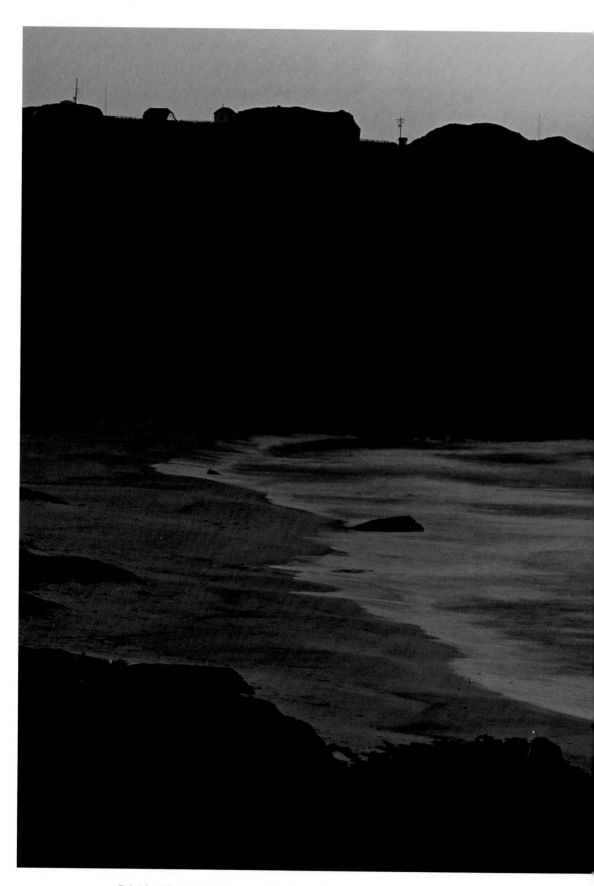

Point Sur Light Station has warned mariners off the rocky coast since 1889.

(*Continued from page 41*) grow along creek beds. Morning sunlight pinks the tips of waves breaking in the surf; in the evening the dying sun lights a highway across the ocean.

On a high hill overlooking this wild coast, newspaper tycoon William Randolph Hearst (1863-1951) built a palace that almost beggars description. From 1919 to 1947 he and architect Julia Morgan created La Cuesta Encantada ("the enchanted hill") at San Simeon. Now known as Hearst Castle, the estate hosted such luminaries as Cary Grant, Jean Harlow, Clark Gable, George Bernard Shaw, Winston Churchill, and Calvin Coolidge. They were treated to such jaw-dropping spectacles as the Neptune Pool, a 104-foot-long outdoor pool decked with statuary modeled after Roman temples and curving colonnades that frame views of the hills and sea. Blue water still shimmers as though a dripping movie star had just emerged. Hearst was so obsessed with getting things exactly the way he wanted them that he tore out and rebuilt the pool twice before he was satisfied. He would even move huge trees from one location to another, in massive concrete containers—a process that took weeks and cost thousands of dollars.

Palms, orange trees, and exotic flowers appear on every terrace landing as one climbs to the Moorish-style guest cottages. Then there is the staggering castle itself, its twin belfries suggestive of cathedrals Hearst had seen as a ten-year-old on a grand tour of Europe with his mother. But it's all an inventive amalgam of pagan and religious—as long as it was beautiful art, Hearst was interested. His collection of tapestries, sculptures, paintings, and furniture was so extensive and valuable that when he briefly went into debt building the castle, he simply sold some of his stuff— in effect, reshuffling his assets.

A typical day during Hearst's reign did not start with a long lazy lie-in. He wanted people up and about—playing tennis, riding, swimming, visiting the exotic animals in his outdoor zoo. Lunch was at 2:30, and dinner at 8:30. Because he could do whatever he wanted, he used paper napkins and put bottles of ketchup out on the long formal table in the refectory. Heavy drinking was frowned upon. David Niven recalled that "the wine flowed like glue." On Saturday night the guests—and there were always plenty—would watch a movie in the 50-seat theater. Afterwards, some would arrange late-night assignations in the lavish indoor pool. Hearst separated from his wife in the mid-1920s and took up with actress Marion Davies, 34 years his junior. He lived here (and in his other houses around the country) until 1947, then spent

Camping in the Ventana Wilderness near Big Sur, vistors find serenity just off the coast. The steep hills of the Santa Lucia Range are often overlooked by motorists shooting the Pacific highway.

his last four years in Beverly Hills, closer to medical care. He tried but was unable to stop the release of the 1941 film *Citizen Kane*, based loosely on his life.

A few miles north of San Simeon, the beaches of Piedras Blancas have become a thriving elephant seal colony. The wind-whipped cove here was long known as a great spot for windsurfing and kayaking; then in 1990, for unknown reasons, northern elephant seals began hauling out on the sand to molt and breed. The colony now numbers a whopping 11,000 animals, with some 2,000 pups born every year. The total species population numbers over 150,000. Not bad for an animal once thought extinct.

At first glance they look like carcasses baking in the sun, but then a flipper will toss some cooling sand. Or a seal will wriggle to a better place, with very audible snorting and huffing noises. In spring the adults leave, and the weaners have to learn to swim by themselves; the males return in summer to molt. By fall juveniles are hauling out to rest, and in winter the big bulls are fighting each other for females. In other words, there are always elephant seals here in one stage or another. In-between times these amazing creatures swim all the way up to Alaska, and they are capable of diving a mile under the surface. They are also not averse to attacking humans who venture too close. Signs warn people to keep their distance, yet curiosity has resulted in a few mangled limbs in recent years. The elephant seal is practically a new phenomenon to locals, so remarkable has been its comeback. As recently as the mid-1990s, the only reliable place to see elephant seals in California was on a tightly controlled guided tour of the rookery at Año Nuevo State Reserve south of San Francisco.

The coast from Piedras Blancas to Carmel is a spectacular series of rock-walled coves and precipitous canyons. Known as the Big Sur coast, this dramatic stretch is ribboned with a twisting two-lane highway clinging to cliffs that overlook the vast Pacific. Rock falls and mudslides sometimes close the road. Tucked away in this mind-altering region are such standbys as the Esalen Institute and Nepenthe. For 40 years Esalen has been offering an "Olympics of the body, mind, and spirit." Anyone with a couple thousand extra dollars, who doesn't mind sharing a room, can spend a week here studying self-aware consciousness. The popular Nepenthe restaurant, a favorite of writers Henry Miller and Jack Kerouac, serves overpriced food with wonderful views on the site where a cabin owned by Orson Welles and Rita Hayworth once stood.

Also along here are pocket parks like the lovely Julia Pfeiffer Burns State Park, where a cliffside trail winds around to a view of a hidden cove some 300 feet below. A waterfall showers from a break in the cliff. On the beach far below, when I visited, someone had fashioned a peace sign in shells. Surrounding the trail is a garden of

Schoolchildren get a feel for tide-pool life near Monterey Bay. One thing they learn is not to pry an animal off a rock—starfish, sea urchins, and others can tolerate only so much handling.

palms, cedars, succulents, purple thistles, and wild daisies, all accompanying an ocean that seems too beautiful to be real.

One of the most stunning of these cliff-and-cove parks on the entire coast lies just south of Carmel. Point Lobos State Reserve is a photographer's dream of rocky tide pools, wildflowery meadows, and rugged promontories leaning into the wind-driven sea. Barking sea lions pull out on slippery rocks; sea otters crack open crabs, using their bellies as tables; cormorants and pelicans dive for food; human divers marvel at the towering forests of kelp beneath the surface. Several trails meander across the headlands, where brush rabbits scamper from the underbrush and gnarled Monterey cypresses frame indelible views of the coast and the Carmel mission.

DEFINING THE SOUTHERN END of Monterey Bay, the Monterey Peninsula holds the bustling communities of Carmel-by-the-Sea, Monterey, and Pacific Grove. Artists and writers had been setting up camp in Carmel since the early 1900s. By mid-century they and other lovers of natural beauty were streaming into Monterey as well, in the backwash

Visitors to the Monterey Bay Aquarium marvel at a three-story-high kelp forest;
seawater comes from the bay just outside.

of the area's declining canning industry. Carmel's little downtown is now chockablock with pricey shops and boutiques on an avenue that leads right down to a sandy beach.

The town got its start up on a bluff in 1771. That's when the Mission San Carlos Borroméo de Carmelo was built. One of the most beautiful in the mission chain, the Carmel mission's courtyard garden, stone church, and Moorish bell tower cry for oil on canvas. Mission-chain founder Padre Junipero Serra chose this as his permanent residence; after his death here in 1784 he was buried beneath the floor in front of the altar. Walking the cloisters with their climbing vines and vaulted roofs, one feels bathed in tranquility.

In the 1830s sailor Richard Henry Dana visited the area on a two-year hide-purchasing stint from Boston. Monterey has grown a lot since then, but many modern travelers would agree with his assessment that Monterey "is decidedly the pleasantest and most civilized-looking place in California." The good weather, the lush vegetation, the setting on a curving bay have all conspired to make this a favorite of visitors over the years. In fact, this book's photographer maintains that if he could choose any place to live on the coast it would probably be Monterey.

The best way to get to Monterey from Carmel is by a detour. Rimming the stubby peninsula, the 17-Mile Drive is an old toll road that takes in unparalleled views of coves, sea-lion rocks, mission-style mansions, and the stately Pebble Beach Golf Links with its world-famous water hazards. Among natural features, the Lone Cypress has been clinging to its rocky outcrop for more than 250 years. Well away from its forest relatives, it stands like a pioneer at the edge of the sea. The 17-Mile Drive is proof that it takes a lot of money and care to make the natural and the man-made flow harmoniously together on a large scale.

The capital of Alta California under the Spanish and Mexicans, Monterey has preserved a number of buildings from the early 1800s. In the early 20th century the town was known for its many sardine canneries. Nobel Prize-winner John Steinbeck immortalized the roughneck character of the place in his 1945 novel *Cannery Row*. After World War II the sardine population suddenly plunged—as likely from natural cycles as overfishing—and by the 1960s most of the canneries were vacant. Yet Cannery Row and Fisherman's Wharf are busier than ever, their taffy shops, ice creameries, galleries, and restaurants catering to an endless supply of tourists. One of the best aquariums on the West Coast, and for that matter in the world, commands a wharfside

Backdrop to many a television show and commercial, the 1872 Pigeon Point Lighthouse ranks as the second tallest on the California coast at 115 feet. The light is visible 20 miles out at sea.

Every year thousands of migrating monarch butterflies, some from as far away
as Canada, winter on pines and eucalyptus trees in Pismo Beach.

A touch of elegance at a bed and breakfast adds another dimension to the youthful flavor of funky Santa Cruz, where standard attire is a tank top, cutoffs, and sandals.

view of the bay and its seabirds and sea otters. The Monterey Bay Aquarium successfully combines gee-whiz thrills with conservation-minded education in a facility brilliantly designed to immerse visitors in various marine environments. A highlight is the one-million-plus-gallon indoor ocean, in which giant tuna, sea turtles, barracuda, and sharks swim past the biggest window on the continent.

On the northwestern tip of Monterey Peninsula, the Victorian-era town of Pismo Beach welcomes tens of thousands of black-and-orange monarch butterflies every year. Migrating from the Pacific Northwest, they have for many years spent October to February here festooning the eucalyptus and pine trees. The amazing thing is that each year the butterflies find their way here even though they are four generations removed from the ones who wintered the previous year.

The Monterey Bay area has become so popular that rush-hour traffic between Monterey and Santa Cruz can be hellacious. After weaving through cars, little towns, and big fields of artichokes, one enters the funky college town of Santa Cruz and breathes a sigh of relief.

A final hymn to Southern California, Santa Cruz revels in its vibrant beach life. Skateboarders, surfers, beach volleyballers, beach bums, career bums, and assorted others have washed up in this freewheeling jumble of freaky and refined. A walk along the beach indicates what's important here—a skateboard park, bikini and surf shops, hole-in-the-wall Mexican restaurants, a surfing museum, and the Santa Cruz Beach Boardwalk. A sign on the dashboard of a car at the skateboard park reads, "Attention meter reader. I put all the change I had into the machine. Please spare me." In summer the boardwalk is a half-mile frenzy of rides, hot-dog stands, funnel cakes, and children. Off-season weekdays it's a ghost town.

The place to go then is Pacific Avenue, a circus of stores, outdoor vendors, and people. On one corner a potbellied sidewalk preacher reads from a tremendous Bible, on another a casual group of musicians plays for charity. Homeless guys sit on benches trading stories about tents being stolen in cold weather, while a bearded old-timer rides his bike facing backwards and asking people if they're having a good evening. Kids drift down from the campus of the University of California at Santa Cruz; other younger kids appear to have drifted to this edge-of-the-continent outpost from anywhere—everyone looking for something new and real and vital. Santa Cruz might be just the place to find it. ❉

Near the Monterey Bay town of Watsonville, a flower farmer displays an armful of heather. In addition to flowers, the Pajaro Valley is known for its apples, strawberries, and artichokes.

redwood coast

Morning fog blankets Mendocino County's coastline.

Northern California

"Punta de los Reyes . . . God help the hapless mariner who drifts upon her shores!" proclaimed the *San Francisco Chronicle* in 1880. So treacherous were the rocks off this northern California peninsula the local papers supposedly had headlines pre-typeset: "Ship Aground at Point Reyes." Fog that can last for days covers the headlands here nearly one-third of the time, and Point Reyes probably claims title to windiest spot on the entire Pacific coast—40-mile-per-hour winds are common; 133 has been recorded.

Yet come here on a clear day and the view is immense. Some 300 feet below the lighthouse, gray whales breach in a swirling sea, murres perch on sheer cliffs, and gulls swoop over the crashing waves. To the south you can make out the Farallon Islands and San Francisco 20 to 30 miles away, while out in front the encircling ocean gradually disappears into a navy-blue band of vapor indistinguishable from the water. With Point Reyes as one of the most breathtaking promontories, the coast from San Francisco up to Redwood National Park is a series of exclamation points, the one section of the Pacific coast that absolutely calls out for a spin along an acrobatic highway hanging between the mountains and the sea. From San Francisco's historic waterfront to the cliffs and coves of Mendocino County to the ancient forests of the redwoods, this chapter takes in a quintessentially gorgeous shoreline that perhaps more than any other says "Pacific coast."

A work of art and an engineering marvel, the beloved Golden Gate Bridge, portal from San Francisco Bay to the Pacific Ocean, provides a scenic backdrop to outdoor activities all over the Bay Area.

If there is a city in the country that can predictably transform a person for the better, it has to be San Francisco. As author William Saroyan observed, "No city invites the heart to come to life as San Francisco does. Arrival in San Francisco is an experience in living." And listen to what seafarer Richard Henry Dana wrote in *Two Years Before the Mast* about a straitlaced New England preacher back in 1859: "Gone was the downcast eye, the bated breath . . . the watchful gait, stepping as if he felt responsible for the moral universe. He walked with a stride, an uplifted open countenance . . . his voice strong and natural and, in short, he had put off the New England deacon and become a human being."

I recognized in that description a friend of my own who came to the Bay Area from back East a pale, skinny intellectual; within a few years he had become a tanned, strapping master of the waves. "One of the best windsurfing places," he recently told me, "is off Crissy Field, below the Presidio. It's very beautiful and dramatic because of the Golden Gate Bridge, the big container ships, the islands, the tides, the fog."

I was lucky enough to visit this city of hills and bridges and clanging cable cars on a rare spring day when there was no weather at all. No wind, just diamond-clear air, about 72 degrees. It was like walking around in one's living room, except that the living room was a gorgeous city above a sparkling bay. Everyone was wearing a smile. A young woman told me, "Even if I didn't live in a rent-controlled apartment, I'd live here anyway. It's liberal, it's never hot, the beaches are beautiful, and you can drive an hour in any direction and find yourself in a spectacular outdoor setting."

The city itself is spectacular enough. At the end of the peninsula forming the southern lip of the bay, it grew from the mission and presidio (military post) sites chosen by Mexican colonizer Juan Bautista de Anza in 1776. But it was the gold rush of 1849 that made San Francisco really boom. As men and equipment poured into the port town, banks and offices rose to service them, as did brothels and saloons. Skyscrapers went up in the early 1900s, and by century's end the Golden Gate city had totally transformed from a blue-collar port into a multicultural trendsetter and Pacific Rim hub of high finance and international trade, all the while maintaining its aesthetic appeal.

A stroll along Fisherman's Wharf, east of Golden Gate Bridge, gives visitors an eyeful of the city's beauty as well as its maritime heritage. From here there are scintillating views of the Golden Gate, the rugged Marin Headlands, Alcatraz Island, the boat-dotted bay, and the city and its impossibly steep streets. The piers used to be jammed with all kinds of vessels—working boats and passenger steamers, military craft and sailing ships. The San Francisco Maritime National Historical Park, to the west of Fisherman's Wharf, gives a taste of that variety. Docked here are a number of walk-aboard vessels, including the 256-foot *Balclutha*, an 1886 three-masted ship that made 17 voyages around Cape Horn between Europe and California.

From Aquatic Park, playground for kayakers and swimmers, the waterfront to the east passes a series of working piers that jut far into the bay. Souvenir shops, small museums, and seafood eateries vie for attention with cruise lines and private boat owners offering tours of the bay (the latter also offer cheaper rates). Street performers on a given day might include jugglers, musicians, or a silver-suited and -painted hip-hop mime. The most popular tourist attraction on Pier 39 has nothing to do with commerce. Shortly after the earthquake of 1989, sea lions began taking up residence on the floating docks here. With herring readily available and no sharks or swift currents, the Pier 39 colony grew to some 600 sea lions. People who have no expectation of seeing so many big wild animals in a city stroll by and end up staying for an hour or more. The young sea lions play and mock-fight in the water, then flipper out and slide atop adults who mildly complain before lying back in the sun. Nearby, grebes and long-necked cormorants dive for mussels, fish, and barnacles.

It's not all tourism on the water. Farther around the Embarcadero, the main waterfront avenue, the piers become more businesslike. The port of San Francisco stays

Only experts need apply: San Francisco's treacherous tides and waves, cold water, and ripping winds challenge windsurfers to their limits. The rewards are thrilling rides with spectacular scenery.

One of the biggest Chinese communities outside Asia, San Francisco's Chinatown stays packed with people, cars, and shops. Its restaurants, gift shops, seafood markets, and produce stands have long attracted curious visitors.

busy around the clock with fish processing, ship repair, warehousing, trucking, cold storage, and more—in all, 7.5 miles of waterfront action. Distinguished by its 235-foot clock tower, the huge 1898 Ferry Building is a hive of activity. Still a ferry terminal, the building is now also a skylit festival marketplace with a tearoom, wine bar, and dealers of gourmet cheeses, meats, mushrooms, olive oil, coffee, and organic fruits. The blended aromas are heavenly. At adjacent Pier 1, men and women in business suits hurry in and out of the port headquarters building, but even here there's a mix—on the end of the pier an old couple throws trail mix to a herring gull, a woman in a Vietnamese hat fishes, and a bare-chested longhaired biker does *tai ji quan* in the sun.

The classic evening view of San Francisco is from the Top of the Mark, the deco-style bar atop the InterContinental Mark Hopkins Hotel, which itself stands on 325-foot-high Nob Hill. The bar is famous for its 100 martinis, with names like Coral Reef and Hanky Panky, and its fabulous circular vistas of skyline and bay. With a martini buzz, "Do You Know the Way to San Jose?" playing softly in the background, and constellations of lights coming on all over the city, it's impossible to go away in a bad mood. (Continued on page 72)

The past blending into the present, San Francisco's colorful cable cars remain a quintessential city sight. Since 1872 the cars have transported people along the city's hilly streets.

Sunset casts a soft glow on Ocean Beach, a three-mile strand on San Francisco's western side.
The beach is popular with brave surfers able to withstand the chilly water and tricky currents.

Pastel houses of San Francisco's Richmond District, north of Golden Gate Park, step down toward the ocean. The district was developed in the late 19th century from an area of rolling sand dunes.

From the headlands of Marin County, Sausalito and the north corner of San Francisco Bay sparkle in evening dress. Upscale Sausalito holds some of the finest houses and gardens in the Bay Area.

(Continued from page 64)

Spanning 1.7 miles, the orange-painted Golden Gate Bridge shoots over the mouth of the bay to the Marin Headlands. The graceful suspension bridge was completed in 1937, and now is used by 115,000 vehicles a day, plus numerous pedestrians. Viewing points on either side provide dramatic vantages, particularly on warm summer afternoons when a continent of white fog can roll in from the ocean, pass through the Golden Gate, and station itself over the bay and city. This frequent phenomenon occurs when cold offshore water chills the humid air above and condenses into fog; the fog brings an ocean-cooled freshness that locals consider natural air conditioning.

Coastal fog is important to the growth of redwoods, accounting for 25 to 50 percent of their water needs. In a secluded canyon 12 miles north, Muir Woods holds the only intact stand of old-growth redwoods in the San Francisco Bay Area. A congressman saved the grove from logging by buying it in 1905 and donating it to the federal government. Theodore Roosevelt proclaimed it a national monument three years later. Conservationist John Muir was pleased: "This is the best tree-lover's monument that could possibly be found in all the forests of the world." The world's tallest living things, California coast redwoods covered more than 2 million acres of the state a few centuries ago; less than 8 percent of those ancient forests remain.

The Muir Woods is a magical place in the early morning, glints of sunlight barely penetrating into this cool forest of giants. Ferns, mosses, and lichens are among the few plants able to live on the choked-out light of the forest floor. The thick spongy bark of trees more than 30 feet wide at the base and 250 feet high dampen the sounds of footsteps, birds, and Redwood Creek. Stare straight up the spiraling grooves and it may be ten stories or more before the eye comes to a branch. In some cases, two trees are fused together, generally the result of a secondary tree sprouting from a burl (a mass of buds) in the first tree.

Surrounding Muir Woods, Mount Tamalpais State Park covers the steep flanks of Mt. Tam, as locals know it. Within the park's 6,300 acres, fir- and redwood-lined canyons rise to ridges covered with chaparral and California laurel; in open grasslands poppies, iris, and shooting stars burst out in spring. Deer, bobcats, and great horned owls find refuge here. But the magnificent views are what draw people, especially to the 2,298-foot peak up a narrow, twisting road. The entire Bay Area lies open at one's feet—the city, its bridges, and inlets lie dozing amid the misty hills, while the Pacific spreads to the west and Mount Diablo rises in the east.

Not far north, the Point Reyes Peninsula owes much of its current profile to the big earthquake of 1906. The triangle of land now occupied by the Point Reyes National

North of Point Reyes, the edge of the continent projects like ship prows into the Pacific Ocean. The coastal highway zigzags high above the rocks and coves, often affording sublime views.

Seashore sits on the eastern edge of the Pacific tectonic plate and moves northwest only about an inch or two a year. The North American and Pacific plates grind together along the San Andreas fault zone, where tremendous pressures build up. In the 1906 cataclysm, the Pacific plate jolted 20 feet forward, opening up finger-like Tomales Bay, which lies directly over the San Andreas Fault. Five million years ago, the peninsula was near Monterey Bay; its present course puts it someday in the Gulf of Alaska.

Drakes Bay would not have looked much different in 1579, when English adventurer Francis Drake likely sailed in for a five-week ship-repairing stint. Local Miwok Indians helped out by supplying the seafarers with boiled fish and wild-root meal. It was another 200 years before settlers arrived, not until the discovery of San Francisco Bay, whose narrow, fog-shrouded entrance had eluded detection. Thus what is now a nearly deserted bay was known long before one of the greatest natural harbors in the world, a mere 15 miles away.

The peninsula is a pleasing mosaic of hilly forests, salt marshes, windswept moors, rocky promontories, and white sand beaches. Small tule elk graze the meadows, sea lions sun on wave-lashed rocks, and some 390 species of birds find niches here. The main road through the park passes the fishing village of Inverness, then winds

through a pastoral landscape dotted with cattle ranches dating from the 1850s. Side roads branch out to several lonely beaches, like the pristine Limantour Spit, a long strand where harbor seals haul out in spring and willets probe the sand with long beaks; back on the lagoon side, snowy egrets stalk the shallows for fish and other prey.

The main road ends after 20 miles at the 1870 lighthouse, which stands on a rocky projection more than 300 feet *below* the headland, an advantage on days when fog rolls high over the sea. On clear days the foghorn sounds about every 20 seconds; on foggy days, it's a nearly perpetual signal, moaning plaintively of danger in a swirling gray void.

About halfway back up the road, I recently stopped at one of several oyster farms in the area and talked with one of the owners—a blond, mid-30s third-generation oysterman. Actually, *he* talked . . . and talked, entertaining me with stories of oyster-eating contests and oyster farming. And his ancestors. He pointed at a rottweiler lying by a washbasin, and said it was his grandfather, reborn as a dog. His grandfather yelled at him, so now he can yell back.

Pacific oysters grow wild in the tidal mudflats of places like Drakes Estero and Tomales Bay, but most farmers produce reliable, tasty oysters by rope culture—the spat (young oysters) are attached to ropes suspended by floats in deep water. The farms consist of a few whitewashed wooden shucking sheds and piles of shells out by a backwater. Shuckers, often Mexican, pry open the shells and put the meat in jars. But they're best right out of the shell. At some places, such as the Tomales Bay Oyster Company, you can buy a dozen oysters (priced by size) and, at picnic tables on the edge of the bay, open them yourself for a real taste of the Pacific coast—salty, succulent, and delicious. People who prefer them cooked bring their own grills.

HIGHWAY 1 TO THE NORTH soon becomes a heart-quickening roller coaster twisting high above the Pacific. Thankfully there are many pullovers to allow motorists and bicyclists a chance to catch a breath of ocean-fresh air and savor incomparable views of vertiginous green hills nosing into a sea too vast to comprehend. (Though there's little traffic along here, pulling over also gets the inevitable one or two speed-crazed drivers off your back.) Gnawing at the coastline *(Continued on page 82)*

The masts of sailboats punctuate a view of Tiburon, a San Francisco bedroom community across the water from Sausalito. Ferries link these bay towns to each other and to the city.

The golden light of sunset finds a deserted beach at Point Reyes National Seashore, where headlands, hillsides, moors, and marshes mingle to create stunning scenes, both far and close (opposite). The first European footprints on the Point Reyes Peninsula were reputedly made by explorer Francis Drake.

Near Trinidad, California, the melting sun lights a path across the ocean and through an arched rock. Battered by an incessantly pounding sea, cliffs give way to isolated rocks like these.

In a forgotten part of Humboldt County, skirted by the Pacific Coast Highway, a student (above) at a counterculture school in Petrolia learns by interacting with the natural world. Likewise a sunhatted boy (opposite) dries seaweed in the quiet erstwhile timber town of Elk.

(Continued from page 75) over several millennia, the Pacific has left many huge, wave-worn rocks, jutting from the ocean like islands and peaks; marine mammals and seabirds populate many of these striking monoliths.

Marine mammals attracted the Russians, who built Fort Ross north of present-day Jenner in 1812 as an area to grow crops to feed Russian settlements in Alaska. Now a state park and national historic landmark, the fort site perches on a high bluff, or coastal terrace, above the ocean. Some 25 Russians and 80 native Alaskans—recruited for their hunting skills—settled this southernmost outpost of the Russian-American Company. By 1820 hunting had nearly wiped out the sea otters, and by the end of the 1830s the Russians had sold their holdings and moved out. But their contributions to the study of local geography, hydrography, botany, and other sciences were invaluable to succeeding generations of Californians. A wooden palisade and cannon-bearing blockhouses were put up to defend against possible Spanish attack. The reconstructed buildings with sea views give a glimmer of frontier life in what is still, more or less, the middle of nowhere.

Just up the coast beyond Point Arena, the charming little town of Mendocino may look familiar to many new arrivals. The town has served as a backdrop for several films and television shows, including *Murder, She Wrote*. In that series, Mendocino stood in for a Maine seaside town. The rugged shoreline was a perfect match, as were the New England-style houses, built by northeasterners in the late 19th century. They came with the lumber boom, which lasted into the 1920s. With the virgin redwood forests depleted in the area, people began to leave; the mill closed in 1938, and the town withered. Then in the late 1950s artists began discovering the aesthetic attraction of the place and the ever changing light and colors on the wildflower-strewn headlands and the sandy beach where the Big River empties into the sea. The whole town is now on the National Register of Historic Places. Quaint shops, restaurants, and inns cater to visitors, and Mendocino Headlands State Park preserves the bluffs from development. Artists still work and sell their canvases in the area. And of further delight to unsuspecting newcomers is the presence of Anderson Valley, just to the southeast. The eight or nine wineries in this sunny vale produce wines on a par with those over in the more well-known Napa.

The *Mendocino Coast Botanical Gardens* is a delightful little Eden set atop bluffs overlooking the rocky coves a few miles north. In spring the rhododendrons burst into color, as do the camellias, daffodils, flowering plums, magnolias, and Pacific coast iris. Migrating birds stop over on northward journeys. In summer and fall, the begonias and fuchsias take over; in winter Japanese maples, heathers, and more than

Mood indigo: With a misty beach for a foreground, the Point Reyes Peninsula ramps down to the Pacific. Halfway up the 600-foot promontory, the lighthouse shines like the eye of a great leviathan.

a hundred varieties of mushrooms paint delicate features in this wonderful setting.

A short trail leads out past carefully maintained flower beds, through a deer-proof fence, to a wilder area, where cypresses form an archway that touches the edge of the bluff. A bright blue Steller's jay quarrels at the intrusion of an early morning visitor, mist swirling from a cypress branch as it flies away. On the headlands, the pungent salty odor of dried kelp arises from the cove below. All around native wildflowers and grasses carpet the bluff. In some cases they have had to be planted to replace invading exotics like the beautiful ice plant that grows all along the northern California coast, its anemone-like purple and yellow blooms seeming anything but aggressive.

North of the lumber and fishing town of Fort Bragg, the Pacific Coast Highway (Highway 1) again becomes a breathtaking slalom course with splendid views from high up. Then the highway mysteriously leaves the coast for about 80 miles. What's out there between "Rockport" (nonexistent, though still on maps) and the Eel River? This rugged land of steep-walled gorges, swift creeks, and desolate rocky beaches was too impenetrable for a north-south highway; in fact, only two narrow, twisting paved roads make it all the way to the coast. The area was logged long ago, the remains of little communities left to rot in the foggy dense forest. Hiking trails cross some of the wilderness of the "Lost Coast" in the southern section, particularly in the Kings Range National Conservation Area and Sinkyone Wilderness State Park.

The vacation community of Shelter Cove is an oddity in the midst of this wild coastline, but it's small and contained, and, sitting at the end of a road, makes for a destination. Tide pools here shelter starfish, abalone, octopus, and limpets, as well as oystercatchers and other birds that live on seafood. The town's remoteness has made it vulnerable over the years to real-estate scams. Recently, speculators have been purchasing lots on streets far too steep to build on; they then promote "beachfront property" on the Internet to unsuspecting buyers.

※

BACK ON THE MAIN COASTAL HIGHWAY, the route from Leggett to Eureka runs about 20 miles from the coast. This is redwood country, and many stands of old-growth forest persist in all their ancient vertical splendor. The spectacular 32-mile Avenue of the Giants tunnels through the largest remaining stand of virgin redwoods in the world. With Woody Guthrie playing on my radio, I drove through recently, enchanted by the patterns of diffracted sunlight—painting the boles of huge trees here, obscuring the thread of road there. This is a forest that invites one to get out and explore. I measured the girth of one venerable titan with my outstretched arms—it took eight lengths to get back around to my starting place. It's humbling not just to imagine these trees being here long before white settlement, but to imagine many of them still standing three centuries or more in the *future*.

Along the road runs the deep green Eel River, its wide gravel banks making a good place to picnic in the sun and study the tree-clad hills all about. From October to February king and silver salmon muscle their way upstream, followed by steelhead trout until April. Within Humboldt Redwoods State Park, the Rockefeller Forest, about halfway along, contains 10,100 acres of the tallest trees around—many soaring over 300 feet. They average 400 to 600 years old, but can live for more than 2,000 years; their resistance to fire and decay makes redwoods remarkably durable. And they are among the fastest growing softwoods, capable of shooting up several feet in a single year. A nearby grove held the champion coast redwood—362 feet tall and 52 feet in circumference—before it fell in 1991.

One tireless champion of the redwoods, Charles Kellogg (1868-1949) was widely

Girls from an alternative school in Redway traipse through a forest. Far removed from urban centers, the remote beaches of southern California have long attracted seekers of a utopian lifestyle.

Youthful exuberance prevails at Arcata's North Country Fair. The presence of Humboldt State University, as well as the entrenchment of hippies since the 1960s, gives Arcata a nonconformist attitude. Yet scenes like the Saturday Farmer's Market (opposite) attest to locals' industry.

known as the "Nature Singer." He claimed to have a twelve-and-a-half-octave vocal range, and a larynx similar to a bird's that enabled him to reproduce bird songs with amazing accuracy. In a mobile home made from an enormous section of redwood mounted to a 1917 Nash Quad truck, the eccentric Kellogg took his vaudeville-style show on the road—whistling, putting out fire with his voice, making fire with sticks, using a divining rod. Recordings of his voice sound indistinguishable from birdcalls. But he is appreciated most for his efforts, in his words, "to awaken interest in the great redwood forests of California, and to assist in their preservation." His mobile home, the "Travel Log," crossed the country four times, and now stands on display in the Humboldt Redwoods State Park visitor center.

Along and near the Avenue of the Giants several old-fashioned tourist traps offer a nostalgic dose of mid-20th-century kitsch. Chimney Tree, Trees of Mystery, Tree House, and more than one "Drive-Thru Tree"—with hand-hewn openings that weaken the tree—ballyhoo weird variations on the area's greatest natural resource. One thing they almost all sell in their gift shops is carved redwood and redwood burls, in the shapes of whales, bears, Bigfoots, and life-size Indians.

Perhaps the most celebrated redwood lover in recent years, Julia Butterfly Hill lived for two years in the branches of a 1,000-year-old redwood south of Eureka. The tree stands on property logged by the Pacific Lumber Company, which finally agreed that if Hill would leave and pay them $50,000 they would preserve the tree, as well as a 200-foot buffer zone. Her supporters from around the world ponied up, and she came down in December 1999. Less than a year later, a vandal chainsawed nearly halfway through the tree. The *San Francisco Chronicle* quoted Hill: "I feel this … as surely as if the chain saw was going through me." The placement of bolts may help protect the tree through at least some storms. In the meantime, the struggle continues between those who see the forest as a cathedral and those who see it as a job.

In the midst of redwood country, Eureka, with a population of 29,000, ranks as the state's largest coastal town north of San Francisco. The large, enclosed Humboldt Bay made the area well suited for a port. Founded in 1850, the town began prospering with the activities of miners, fishermen, and loggers. Within five years, some 140 schooners were hauling lumber from the bay and 7 mills buzzed along its banks. Several fish- and-whale processing facilities operated on the bay. The opening of the Northwestern Pacific Railroad in 1914 gave Eureka an inland link with San Francisco and added to the city's prosperity.

Elegant Victorian-style houses from Eureka's boom times still grace the city's streets. The most ornate, the olive-hued Carson Mansion was built in 1885 by lumber baron William Carson; it now serves as a private club. The turreted Pink Lady opposite, though smaller, is nearly as ostentatious. I spent a recent night in an 1888 gingerbread-trimmed landmark proudly named "Abigail's Elegant Victorian Mansion." It deserves the name. What with chiming grandfather clocks, brocaded wall coverings, period furniture, pull-chain commodes, a Victrola, and a collection of silent movies, this place breathes Victoriana in every cozy treasure-filled nook. My garrulous host, northern California native and former merchant seaman Doug Vieyra likewise filled the air with commentary on local history and personalities. He said guests from warmer climes sometimes call ahead, concerned that the mansion has no air-conditioning. When they arrive he tells them, "It's just a little different from what you're used to." He then opens a window and a predictably cool evening breeze wafts in from the bay.

Down near the bay along Second Street run five or six blocks of craft galleries, bookshops, cafes, and restaurants. A concrete "boardwalk" off First strolls along the bay within hailing distance of the Woodley Island marina. The whole effect is of an old lumber town catering to tourists but with an unstudied effortlessness. There are still plenty of working-class houses, kids on skateboards, and an unapologetic view of a pulp mill downriver. Some 300 fishing vessels continue to operate out of Humboldt Bay, bringing in piles of salmon, rockfish, Dungeness crab, shrimp, and oysters.

The rustic Samoa Cookhouse out on the north spit dates from the area's rough-and-tumble logging days. Three hearty meals are still served daily lumber-camp-style at long tables with slick checkered cloths. Though spruced up, the place still has an authentic atmosphere, enhanced by its displays of old saw blades and logging-camp equipment. But the Café Marina back on Woodley Island has the better view. I feasted here on grilled oysters dockside, watching gulls wheel above working and pleasure craft. At the end of the marina stands a memorial to area fishermen lost at sea, erected by the fishermen's wives of Humboldt County. A stone tablet lists 64 names from 1936 to 1999, stars by most names indicating bodies not recovered. There is plenty of room for more names. A giant bronze carving of a fisherman with his net stands in the shallows, where willets poke the silt for dinner. Sundown paints the water in tones of amber and slate, and bathes downtown Eureka across the channel in rose.

The other main town on Humboldt Bay, Arcata has a laid-back sophistication created in part by artists and hippies who have prospered here over the last few decades. The town started as a mining supply center around the same time as Eureka, and boasts a fair number of Victorian houses. The founding of Humboldt State University in 1913 ensured Arcata a youthful energy. One of the prides of local citizens, the remarkable Arcata Marsh and Wildlife Sanctuary is also known as the waste-reclamation project. That's because this innovative series of ponds and marshes was landscaped both to reclaim an industrial area for wildlife and to filter city sewage. The 250 species of birds here attest to the project's success, as do the city planners and engineers who come from far and wide to study it. Hikers and bird-watchers take to the five miles of trails that wind through the 275-acre sanctuary.

Another fine outdoor spot located a short distance up the coast, Patrick's Point State Park has everything a northern California coastal park should. Claiming the precipitous bluffs around rocky Patrick's Point, the park is too close to the sea to have redwoods, but it does have a thick lush forest of spruce, hemlock, fir, rhododendron, and blackberry and huckleberry bushes. Weathered spruces draped with Spanish moss cling to even the narrowest ledges. If not for the trails, getting out to the edge would be a daunting prospect. It's a short but steep walk down to Agate Beach, with a final scramble over jagged white-veined boulders of black basalt. Beachcombers scan for wave-polished translucent stones and bone-smooth driftwood in unusual shapes. Early morning fog is almost a given,   *(Continued on page 96)*

A Mendocino pot grower displays his harvest. Since 1996, the county has allowed card-carrying individuals to grow up to 25 plants for medicinal use.

For the wild and wacky glory of it, participants in the Arcata to Ferndale Kinetic Sculpture Race
attack the competition. The event features weird vehicles racing a course of sand, mud, and water.

A time-lapse shot of San Francisco's Ocean Beach catches moody swirls of fog at sunset.

Ancient giants stretch to the sun in Humboldt Redwoods State Park, home
to some of the tallest trees in the world. Mosses and fungi (above) are among
the few plants that flourish in the deep darkness of the redwood forests.

(*Continued from page 89*) banked in shoals against the lower cliffs, while sunlight fringes the higher reaches.

Another short trail leads down to a view of Mussel Rock—a sea stack shaped like a huge open shell—and a knowledge of why swimming is not advisable in this park. In addition to the cold water and strong undertow, the waves blast against rocks barely visible above the surface, and the occasional "sleeper wave" piles in with sudden tremendous force. But the views are enough. From Wedding Rock and Patrick's Point, the aqua water 200 feet below runs to a glaucous sea beyond the rocks where birds chase fishing boats and migrating whales spout and surface.

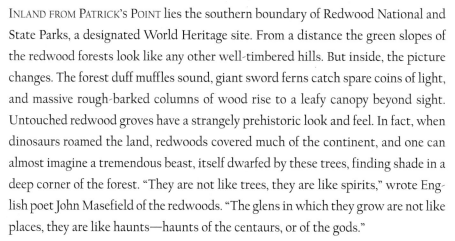

INLAND FROM PATRICK'S POINT lies the southern boundary of Redwood National and State Parks, a designated World Heritage site. From a distance the green slopes of the redwood forests look like any other well-timbered hills. But inside, the picture changes. The forest duff muffles sound, giant sword ferns catch spare coins of light, and massive rough-barked columns of wood rise to a leafy canopy beyond sight. Untouched redwood groves have a strangely prehistoric look and feel. In fact, when dinosaurs roamed the land, redwoods covered much of the continent, and one can almost imagine a tremendous beast, itself dwarfed by these trees, finding shade in a deep corner of the forest. "They are not like trees, they are like spirits," wrote English poet John Masefield of the redwoods. "The glens in which they grow are not like places, they are like haunts—haunts of the centaurs, or of the gods."

Here in the northwest corner of California, Redwood National and State Parks protect nearly half the remaining old-growth redwoods. It was only about 150 years ago that the redwoods forests were unknown to the ax. But with miners and other settlers pushing into the region, the trees began looking like timber—in other words, like money. Logging camps mushroomed around the forest, complete with choppers, sawyers, cooks, and road builders. These Paul Bunyans would first prepare a bed of small trees to catch the falling giant so it would not shatter. Two expert choppers with three-pound axes hacked out a V-shape in the trunk, positioning it so that the tree would fall in the intended direction. A two-man saw on the other side bit through deep enough to topple the tree, and down it would come with a ground-shaking explosion. Peelers then stripped off the bark with long iron bars, and the wood was cut into sections to be dragged away by teams of oxen or draft horses.

In the first half of the 20th century, power saws, tractors, and bulldozers made logging more rapid and efficient and enabled the industry to claw into the most rugged sections of the forest. In this way the great redwood forests succumbed to the need and greed of an expanding nation. Founded in 1918, the Save-the-Redwoods League began to raise concern about the loss of a national treasure; with private donations it bought the land that started three state parks. In the early 1960s the National Geographic Society chipped in money to survey a site for a possible national park, and in 1968 Redwood National Park was born. But with logging continuing on adjacent land, erosion was dumping so much sediment into the creeks that they were overflowing downstream and threatening protected groves. It was clear that the Redwood Creek watershed needed protection. In 1978 Congress expanded the park boundaries to protect the lower third of the Redwood Creek watershed. Redwood National and State Parks now measure 105,000 acres.

The southern part of the park contains some of the loftiest trees in the world, and also the most difficult to get to. An 8-mile hiking trail takes determined hikers into the remote Tall Trees Grove, but then they have the same distance to walk back. A steep 16-mile road (about half of it unpaved) is the only other way in, but there's still a nearly 3-mile roundtrip hike to the grove and back. There are, however, plenty of splendid groves not far off the highway, with ancient trees topping 300 feet. And from the ground you really cannot tell the difference between 300 and 360 feet. The nature trail behind Prairie Creek Redwoods visitor center, for instance, traipses among skyscrapers, the understory scented with California bay trees (pepperwoods).

In Jedediah Smith Redwoods State Park, this steelhead trout will soon grace a plate. Unlike salmon, steelhead make more than one trip from the ocean to their spawning ground and back.

Wild for the waves, an eager surfer dashes into the ocean at Redwood National Park's Crescent Beach. Some 35 miles of untamed coastline rims the western edge of this grand park.

Tree burls take fantastic shapes. These knobby protuberances can sprout if a tree is stressed by fire or other damage, thus giving redwoods an extra strategy for survival. The redwood's cone belies its potential. Only one inch long, the 60-120 seeds in each cone may produce 360-foot giants that tower over all other forest life.

Black bears and mountain lions still thrive in the redwood forests, as do Roosevelt elk, saved from the edge of extinction. Other species facing an uphill climb include the northern spotted owl and the marbled murrelet. A threatened seabird that nests on the branches of old-growth redwoods and other high conifers, the murrelet is one of the strangest creatures around, its habits still not fully known. Instead of staying on the coast, it zooms back and forth from forest to sea—up to 52 miles—several times a day to bring food to its one annual chick. A diving bird, it comes in like a bullet at up to 86 miles per hour, practically crashing into the

trees, and lands on its mossy nest. Not a great adaptive strategy in the modern world, but it's what they do.

"It's an indicator species," says Maria Mudd Ruth, who is writing a book on the murrelet. "When you've got a bird associated with an endangered habitat—the old-growth forest—and the marine environment where tanker traffic and commercial fishing is heavy, you've got a double whammy. Everything from oil spills and gill-net fishing to logging and development affects it. Even though you might never see this bird, its loss means the loss of things you can see and do value."

Redwood National and State Parks also protect 37 miles of cove-bitten shoreline. Tide pools shelter the likes of sea stars, giant green anemones, and sea urchins, and the Klamath River estuary entertains fishermen and kayakers. The boundary extends a quarter mile offshore, the zone in which gray whales migrate in winter and spring. Thick mats of kelp rocking in the swells can look like sea lions nosing the surface—plenty of marine mammals do inhabit these parts. And salmon and steelhead still swim unimpeded up the Smith River, in the north part of the park—the last major undammed river in California.

✺

JUST BELOW CRESCENT CITY, in the northwest corner of the state, a wide curving beach extends for several miles. It's not unusual on warm days, even in early spring, to see a line of cars parked just off the road and scores of people sunning on this inviting sandy beach. Surfers and swimmers take advantage of these balmy days—the water is never going to get much higher than 55 degrees anyway, and the ocean here can be relatively calm. Yet up near the lighthouse at the north end of the crescent, jagged sea stacks look like ships cresting the water as waves smash against them.

Highway signs around here and all the way into Washington warn coastal travelers that this is a tsunami zone. Although extremely rare, these tidal waves can rise to monstrous proportions. The last bad one occurred in Crescent City in March of 1964. An earthquake in Alaska sent seismic waves rolling southwest at 500 miles per hour. They hit the shore here in the middle of the night, clogging the streets with logs and debris. People came out to see what was happening and to help clean up. Then two more waves piled in. But it was the fourth wave that made citizens realize how dangerous a tsunami can be. A 21-foot-tall wall of water bulldozed the town, collapsing power lines, tossing cars and buildings about like playthings, and destroying 29 city blocks. When it was over, 11 people were dead. Coastal residents now understand that when the ground trembles, they need to get in their cars and drive east until they are at least 100 feet above sea level, then stay there until officials declare the coast safe.

But few locals worry about tsunamis and other natural catastrophes. They're a small price to pay for living and vacationing along this ruggedly beautiful section of the West Coast. After all, they happen maybe once in a generation, not every year like Atlantic coast hurricanes. And while winter gales can be fierce and summer fog thick, they simply add to the brooding appeal of a region where the human population is far less evident than the wild things. May the wild things forever own this ribbon of mythic trees and sea-lashed cliffs. ✺

From its rocky perch, Battery Point Lighthouse in Crescent City has been warning mariners off hazardous rocks at the harbor mouth since 1856. The building also holds a small museum.

no wilder shore

Highway 101 traces the coast of southern Oregon.

OREGON

❋

zWAVES CRASH against rugged sea stacks. Murres and cormorants mass on sheer cliffs. Sea lions haul out on beaches littered with driftwood and Japanese glass floats. Fishing trawlers pull into small harbors laden with harvest from the sea.

These scenes are typical of the Oregon coast, a stripe of shoreline stitched together by state parks. Thanks to a 1967 state legislative act, nearly all beaches are in the public domain. A few beach towns on the northern coast have sprawled a bit with vacation homes and traffic, yet most of the wild Oregon edge remains as it has for decades. One measure of the coast's value as a natural corridor, the recent completion of the Oregon Coast Trail means hikers can now walk the entire distance from California to Washington.

Way on the southern end of the Oregon coast, the small town of Brookings lies within the "banana belt." Not that bananas are grown here, but Oregon likes to tout this region's climate as an antidote to its cold and rainy reputation. Winter temperatures here can climb into the 70s, and Brookings cultivates up to 90 percent of the country's Easter lilies. But Brookings is perhaps best known for being the target of the only bombing of the United States mainland in World War II. On September 9, 1942, a tiny plane assembled on the deck of a Japanese submarine flew over the forest east of town and dropped a bomb. The idea was to start a forest fire, but wet conditions made it easy for firefighters to handle.

On a pier in Bandon, cooked crabs will soon grace plates in a local restaurant. A town of less than 3,000, Bandon is one of numerous fishing villages on Oregon's coast.

The pilot returned 20 years later to present Brookings a samurai sword—handed down through his family for four centuries—as a symbol of reconciliation. In 1992 he returned to plant a redwood tree; finally, after his death in 1997, his wishes were honored with the scattering of some of his ashes on the bomb site.

The Samuel H. Boardman Scenic Corridor a short way up the coast comes as a relief to those traveling the Pacific Coast Highway and seeing no coast after California. A plaque here honors "the father of Oregon state parks," first park superintendent Samuel H. Boardman (1874-1953), for his work in conserving the state's great wilderness areas. He would be pleased with the blufftop view—blue sea surrounding a house-shaped sea stack, with the roar of breakers funneling up a canyon, birds singing from dark green thickets, and butterflies sipping upon wild daisies. The narrow strip of park waysides and viewing areas extends for 12 miles, with fir-clad mountains dropping right into the cliff-edged sea.

To the north, after Cape Sebastian, the shoreline bows inward, so that at Port Orford one can look south and see the cape nearly 30 miles away. At Port Orford's small city park, a tremendous dinosaur-like sea stack called Battle Rock juts from the beach into the sea. The Oregon Donation Land Act gave settlers the gumption to come to these shores and grab parcels of land for themselves. It was on this rock that a party of nine settlers took refuge from besieging Indians in 1851. Not to be discouraged, a more well-armed party of 70 returned a month later and established the settlement that would grow to Port Orford. A few years later most of the area's remaining natives were rounded up and held in pens until they could be deported by steamship north to the Coast Reservation. A final band of holdouts was marched the 125 miles to the reservation.

The westernmost town in the contiguous United States, Port Orford is one of the rainiest on the coast, with 108 inches annually. But with a population of only 1,200, it has a pleasantly small-town feel. Cranberry farming is the area's mainstay, along with sheep farming and tourism. A lack of chain motels or chain restaurants only adds to the area's rough beauty. A park high up on the headlands preserves a lifeboat station that operated here from 1934 to 1970. During that time the local coast guard conducted courageous search-and-rescue missions, and patrolled the waters for enemy craft. Their motto—"You have to go out . . . you don't have to come back"—must have separated the brave from the timid.

One of the most interesting things to do here is to observe the activity down at the dolly dock, one of only a handful in the world. Port Orford has a natural deepwater harbor, yet it is the only port between San Francisco and Seattle with a hoist system for its fishing fleet. The heavy southwest winds make mooring too dangerous, hence the marina has two tremendous 15- and 25-ton hoists to set the fishing boats into the water, and pull them back out onto their trailers again at the end of the day.

I came down one dusk to watch the boats unload their catches. Two fishermen, in waterproof overalls and deck boots, scooped the fish out of the hold, dumped them into baskets, and hosed them off. A dockworker hauled the baskets up by pulley to the weigh station. Salty banter flowed easily between the men, as they complained about the size of the fish and the speed of the operation. "That's a red Irish lord—he's no good, throw him back." The fish went overboard; a sea lion head popped up, and a gull swooped over, as the excitement grew. The fish kept coming up—cabezons, lingcods, Chinas, coppers, blacks—the names as strange as the fish. The weigher wrestled the big ones onto the scales, talking to them: "Hold still now, or you'll be sorry." He then tossed the gasping fish into big bubbly holding tanks. The boat captain motored forward to the hoist. The hoist operator lowered a huge hook, upon which the two fishermen looped four ropes—two from the starboard side, two from the port. Then slowly the boat, with men aboard, rose the 15 or so feet to the level of the marina. The fishermen, fit men in their twenties, hopped out and guided their boat onto the waiting trailer, then spent a few minutes (Continued on page 112)

Calling it a day, fishing boats in Newport Harbor cast reflections on still water. Newport's location on Yaquina Bay makes fishing a big industry in this lively little town.

Goats graze in the Samuel H. Boardman Scenic Corridor, as sundown gilds the ocean around a seastack.

With the blast and spray of waves for accompaniment, a pelican glides along the shore; these diving birds often stray into Oregon and Washington from points south.

Fading into the fog, rocks on the Bandon beach have the appearance of modern
sculpture. Waves eventually wear them away, carving fantastic figures in the process.

Is it a keeper? A crabber and her companion inspect their haul on a Bandon pier, where locals can shop for dinner without cash or credit. A little patience nets tasty results.

readying the vessel for the next outing. "We go out just about every day we can," one told me. "Today we were at the reef near Cape Blanco, about three to five miles out. Usually we'd be out crabbing, but they slow down in April."

To take a look at where they'd been, I drove up to Cape Blanco. The chalky white of the cliffs here, produced by fossilized shells, made for an obvious name when Spanish explorers cruised by. The windswept headland presides over gorgeous rock-studded shorelines that curve north and south. Such views can begin to have a sameness. Variety comes from a number of details—the birds or marine mammals at one place, an oddly shaped rock at another. Here a rock juts up some 50 feet like an old chimney or pagoda; rocks at other coves suggest whales, ships, pinnacles, and bizarre chessmen. There were no fishing vessels within sight at Cape Blanco, but the 1870 lighthouse was open for tours. The red-roofed beacon is only 59 feet tall, but add the 245 feet from water to clifftop and the light is visible for a dozen miles or more at sea. With increasing reliance on Global Positioning System, automated lights, and other technologies, some of Oregon's lighthouses are either nonoperational or no longer use the old Fresnel lenses. The U.S. Coast Guard has been selling the lighthouses off to federal and state agencies for upkeep as historic monuments. But the Cape Blanco still shines as of old, providing a tangible link to the region's maritime past. One can stand on these foggy headlands and imagine a three-masted schooner, loaded with lumber, nosing along the coastline a century ago, watching for the cautionary flash of light.

✳

STORMS ALONG THE OREGON COAST can indeed be monumental, but they are almost always limited to winter. And they have their own aficionados, people who rent a room with a big ocean view, sit back with a drink, and watch the storms pile in with Wagnerian force. Then there are weeks at a stretch in summer when no rain falls at all. Of course, summer fog can close in like a gauzy veil. But year-round mild temperatures prevail. In fact, in some places the water may be warmer in winter than summer because the Davidson Current pushes northward against the prevailing California Current that swings south from Alaska.

Just up the coast, Bandon may not have quite the rustic charm of Port Orford, but it still has its appeal. Though artisans and tourists have discovered the town and its beaches of hard-packed sand, Bandon remains decidedly small-town, best known for its location at the mouth of the Coquille River. On the north side of the river, Bullards Beach State Park fronts a salt marsh of some 800 acres where thousands of waterfowl and shorebirds call in during spring and fall migrations. At the park's south end, the 1896 Coquille River Lighthouse is one of Oregon's shortest at a mere 47 feet. From here you can look across the river to Bandon's old town, or gaze out on the north jetty, with choppy water to either side and a foghorn cutting the air. Up to the right spread miles of sandy beach, perfect for long contemplative walks. Piles of driftwood, some pieces as big as trees, spread along the duneline. Sometimes colorful Japanese fishing floats will wash ashore; these glass globes can spend a decade from the time they break free of their fishing nets until they reach the shore here, thousands of miles away.

Visible to the north, the 100-foot-high bluffs of Cape Arago provide a terrific crow's nest for spying on migrating gray whales. Just about any high headland will do. I came on a clear morning in mid-spring, and had soon counted several spouts. A local volunteer told me that the southward migration, in the winter, is more concentrated; it is possible then to see 30 whales in an hour. But the advantage in

Evening softens the curves of a vintage farm truck in Bandon (above) and the rocky shore at Yachats (right). The tiny town of Yachats is popular for smelt fishing and beachcombing.

spring, from a whale-watcher's point of view, is that currents dictate that the whales swim closer to shore. These amazing 30-ton leviathans make the longest known migration of any mammal, 6,000 miles from the Bering Sea to Mexico. Though hunters nearly drove them to extinction in the late 1800s and early 1900s, they have fully recovered. The entire population is estimated at 21,000, and many of these nearly 50-foot-long whales make the annual migration. Some 400 or so others find the local waters so inviting they stay year-round along the Oregon coast.

A few hundred yards out from the cape, Shell Island and Simpson Reef harbor whole barking, grunting communities of California and Steller sea lions, harbor seals, and elephant seals. The Steller sea lions are larger and paler than their California cousins—a male averages 11 to 12 feet long and weighs about 2,400 pounds. The California is one of the fastest marine carnivores, capable of 25-mile-per-hour bursts; they can dive more than 1,700 feet and stay under for 12 minutes, hunting for squid, abalone, octopus, and fish. Highly vocal, California sea lions are the likely suspects if you hear boisterous barking from the rocks. Unlike the sea lions, harbor and elephant seals have no external ear flaps. Harbor seals are the smaller of the two, with males

Wind-rippled mountains of sand stretch 40 miles along the coast at Oregon Dunes
National Recreation Area.

Exploding through a blowhole, the waves at Cape Perpetua Scenic Area put on a steady show. The rocky shoreline here is among the most dramatic on the entire West Coast.

topping out at more than 370 pounds. The impressive male elephant seal can weigh more than two tons; it is recognizable by its big drooping snout. Their territorial and female-attracting fights can be highly dramatic, their inflated snouts making a bellowing noise audible a mile away. Once hunted for their blubber, elephant seals were down to about 20 individuals on an island off Baja California in the 1890s. After protection, they made a spectacular comeback, and now number more than 150,000.

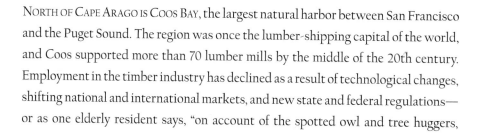

NORTH OF CAPE ARAGO IS COOS BAY, the largest natural harbor between San Francisco and the Puget Sound. The region was once the lumber-shipping capital of the world, and Coos supported more than 70 lumber mills by the middle of the 20th century. Employment in the timber industry has declined as a result of technological changes, shifting national and international markets, and new state and federal regulations— or as one elderly resident says, "on account of the spotted owl and tree huggers,

I guess." With a large retirement community in the area, health care is the biggest industry now, along with tourism. The Pacific Coast Highway passes right through the adjacent waterfront towns of Coos Bay and North Bend, which together create the largest metropolitan area on the Oregon coast. The highway offers a sampling of the way locals have diversified, from the usual stores, motels, and restaurants to a waterside casino that operates out of a former lumber mill. Part-time fishermen offer bay cruises, and big piles of wood chips are now considered nearly as important as logs—loaded onto Japanese factory ships, the chips are mixed with chemicals and turned into low-grade paper.

In the midst of a coastline characterized by rocky bluffs, the 50-mile stretch north of Coos Bay comes as a big surprise. One of the largest dune systems on the West Coast runs along here like a miniature Sahara. Mountains of sand up to 200 feet high, dotted with tree islands and fringed with lithe grasses, form a two- to three-mile barrier between the ocean and the highway. In fact, to see the Pacific along here, you generally need to find your way to the top of one of these dunes. The view from the Oregon Dunes Overlook, for example, is huge. Emerging from the forest, overlapping waves of sand roll down and out for a mile or more, around little water-filled basins, to a buffer of low shrubs, then finally to a wide beach and the sea.

The Oregon Dunes National Recreation Area encompasses most of this impressive system. Some of its dunes measure more than a mile in length, but they are constantly changing in size and shape. Return in a few months and the views will be altered. Wind shifts these giant sand piles the way water carves a canyon, but over a much shorter period of time. These dunes shift an average of three feet in a year.

Recent studies show that the the majority of the new sand coming into the dunes system is introduced through the Umpqua River. In addition, the lack of headlands here allows beach sand to blow inland. The combined action of waves, currents, and tides churns up more offshore sand and deposits it on the beach. Wind can then rob this endless supply and add to the mounds behind. In the summer, steady north and northwest winds blow at about 15 miles per hour; winter winds come from the southwest and can, during storms, pack a 100-mile-per-hour wallop.

In the southern part of the recreation area, the John Dellenback Dunes Trail loops into the most spectacular area, with dunes more than 400 feet above sea level. After a cool green forest of Sitka spruce, hemlock, and Douglas fir, the trail emerges into a range of high dunes that give panoramic vistas of dunes, forest, beach, and ocean. In places the dune slopes bear corduroy patterns, mimicking the rippling movement of the dunes themselves. Another interesting phenomenon, winter winds can carve

In view of the Yaquina Bay Bridge (left), a fishing vessel docks at Newport Harbor. As in a dream,
head-size moon jellies pulse hypnotically through a tank at Newport's Oregon Coast Aquarium,
where most of the 200 species are native to local coastal waters.

a series of thin ridges called yardangs that rise up to 15 feet high. Fascinated by the endless variety of patterns the dunes can take, the sand mounded in smooth curves against a sharp blue sky, I got briefly lost wandering about these open hourglasses. A quick scan from the top of a high dune got me reoriented.

The dune field dips to a deflation plain, a low-lying strip behind the beach where water collects; great egrets and other birds patiently stalk prey in these little lagoons. Winter's heavy rains fill up these low areas, then a light layer of sand blows over the water, making them less easy to see. These patches of quicksand are more of a nuisance than a real danger to hikers, but can be a serious threat to those on off-highway vehicles.

After a long climb to the top of a dune, some people like to snowboard or sled down; others are content to slip and slide in their bare feet. Either way, it's good fun, and a lot less noisy than the OHVs that are allowed to share the recreation area. Those who value a wild wilderness have come in conflict over the years with four-wheeler and dune buggy enthusiasts. Though restricted to certain sections, mostly in the south end, these roaring OHVs can absolutely spoil a peaceful day at the dunes. For now, an uneasy truce exists.

Another problem confronting the Oregon Dunes was a well-intended human intervention of the late 1920s. To keep the shifting dunes from spreading over highways and coastal development, locals in Florence began planting European beach grass. Not only did the hardy species stabilize the dunes, it began spreading south in a line just behind the beaches, where conditions were favorable for its growth. Within a few decades the beach grass had trapped enough sand to create a line of foredunes 20 to 30 feet high. These foredunes now prevent fresh sand from replenishing the main dunes. As these main dunes keep migrating inland, there are no waves of sand to take their place, and the native forest moves in instead. Eventually, unless the beach grass is eradicated, the high dunes will be no more.

✳

NORTH OF THE OREGON DUNES ABOUT 25 MILES, the coast makes yet another dramatic statement. At the Cape Perpetua Scenic Area, the inland Coast Ranges come swooping suddenly down to a crashing sea. The highest point on Oregon's coast reachable by car, the 800-foot-high lookout delivers sweeping views of mountains, sea, and 65 miles of crenellated shoreline. From this high up, the turbulent coast looks like a series of Japanese gardens fringed by lacy waves. Gray whales blow and breach beyond the

Sidewalk whale-watching: Newport's splashy murals spread across several downtown buildings. Along with the sea air, these nautical scenes help local shops and restaurants do a brisk business.

breakers, with seabirds riding their coattails in the search for fish. Some of the area's trails investigate a wonderful old-growth forest of Sitka spruce, while others head down to the beach. One of the latter leads to Cook's Chasm, where water sluices through a long channel of volcanic rock, then bursts through a blowhole with a whale-like spray. An even bigger blowhole, Devils Churn, lies a little farther along. At low tide the tide pools near here are a wader's dream of sea stars, hermit crabs, sea cucumbers, and nudibranchs. The strange nudibranch, or sea slug, is a shell-less mollusk that eats anemones.

On a recent trip up the coast, I learned more about these and other sea creatures at the Oregon Coast Aquarium in Newport. In fact, more than 15,000 creatures live at the aquarium. Seeing them close up, and listening to keepers talk about them, makes one want to go out and see more in the wild. The twice-daily feeding times are among the most interesting, and popular, events here. The sea lions and seals flip, twirl, and leap onto the rocks for fish. Above- and below-water viewing windows give one a chance to study the nuances of these graceful, apparently effortless swimmers. Of the six sea lions and five harbor seals living here when I visited, four were rescued after beach strandings and the others were born in captivity; none would likely survive if released into the wild.

Just as captivating are the four sea otters in a nearby tank. They delight in feeding time, floating on their backs holding shrimp, crabs, *(Continued on page 129)*

A gray mist on the sea's face intensifies sunlit Yaquina Head Lighthouse, built in 1872.

Angling for the big ones, fishermen cast for salmon at Nehalem Bay. In the fall, fish topping as much as 50 pounds surge through here on their way up the Nehalem River to spawn.

Every September Depoe Bay, north of Newport, puts on a Native American-style salmon bake in City Park. The fresh fish are cooked on alder stakes over an open fire, then served with local trimmings.

(Continued from page 123) and clams, devouring the meat and licking out the shells. After a meal they go back to playing with balls and other "enrichment toys." These animals were found as orphans and are likewise not releasable. Weighing less than 100 pounds, sea otters possess a prodigious appetite that calls for a $15,000 annual food bill per otter—enough to equal 25 percent of their body weight a day. Unlike seals, sea otters have no insulating blubber. Instead, they have a thick rich pelt with a million hairs per square inch—more per square inch than on a whole human scalp. They spend up to three hours a day grooming so that their fur will stay waterproof; oil spills render a sea otter's coat useless, leading to hypothermia. It was their fur that nearly spelled doom for the entire species, after heavy hunting up through the early 1900s. The last wild Oregon sea otter was killed in 1906. Protected in 1911, they were rarely seen along the Pacific coast until a herd showed up south of Monterey, California, in 1936; that herd now numbers about 1,000, and larger groups live in Alaskan and Russian waters.

The aquarium's Orford Reef exhibit allows coast travelers the chance to put names to the fish they might have seen fishermen bring in to Port Orford and other places. Cabezon, lingcod, and various rockfish swim all about the walk-through acrylic tunnel in this huge tank. In another even bigger tank, an orca (killer whale) named Keiko once lived. After much public clamor for and against letting him go, the star of the 1993 movie *Free Willy* was released into a bay pen off Iceland in 1998, then four years later into the open ocean. The first captive orca released into the wild, he joined a pod, but died of acute pneumonia after about a year. He was 27 years old. A small exhibit, now removed, memorialized him with letters from fans, including an 11-year-old Oregon girl who wrote, "When I heard that you died I was sad. Keiko I really love you. I hope that you are very happy now."

Newport has been a seaside resort for over a century, and thus not as hard hit by the lumber slump of the last few decades. Though the town now has some strip development along U.S. 101, its old bayfront area moves to a much slower beat. Along here restaurants, shops, and taverns mingle easily with seafood-processing plants. Big sleek sea lions lie out on floating docks in the wharf, barking with their whiskered noses in the air. Gulls walk the decks of fishing trawlers; halyards ping against masts, the boats rocking gently. On nice days the Undersea Gardens and other bayfront "attractions" can hardly compete with what's right outside. Vivid nautical maritime murals splash across old buildings along here. In one a bearded

Preparing for lift-off: A participant in a Lincoln City kite festival launches her entry. Already aloft, spinsocks up to 150 feet long stream across a cobalt-blue sky.

Three Arch Rocks wildlife refuge (above) offshore from Oceanside hosts a tremendous variety of birds and marine animals. At the Ecola State Park beach (right), a boy plays where Lewis and Clark explored—the farthest south they journeyed on the coast.

fisherman rows a small boat, a lighthouse on a rocky promontory in the background, and storm clouds threatening—or perhaps the clouds are moving off east, and, judging from the size of the fish in his boat, the fisherman has gotten away with some good luck. I stopped in the Whale's Tale for a pint of local ale and delicious grilled rock cod topped with fruit salsa; authentic maritime décor enhanced the experience. My waitress told me that the whale jawbone and rib hanging from the ceiling were owned before the ban on collecting marine mammal parts and thus grandfathered in.

Newport's Yaquina Bay Lighthouse makes a fine stand for watching a sunrise or sunset. Views pan from the ocean to the bay, with the 1871 lighthouse in the rear. This little sentinel on a high bluff shone only three years before a brighter one was built just north at Yaquina Head, making this the quickest lighthouse in Oregon to go obsolete. But its usefulness was not quite over. In 1996 the U.S. Coast Guard re-lit it to help vessels navigate through this stretch of coast. Also from this point, the impressive Yaquina Bay Bridge commands attention; the 1930s bridge was the final link in Oregon's coastal highway. Traffic streams across while oceangoing vessels sail underneath, in and out of the harbor. Forming a long chute, jetties on either side keep the harbor from closing up with sand, which has instead piled up in the form of beaches north and south of Yaquina Bay.

※

WHILE NEWPORT may stand accused of sprawl, Lincoln City to the north is guilty as charged. Here, five little towns coalesced into one, and the result is seven miles of highway development. Lincoln City's answer to a gasping economy was to become the proud home of more than 65 factory-outlet stores, as well as a plethora of lesser shops selling crafts, bikes, antiques, and locally made kites. Yet just off the highway, the town is blessed with seven miles of beach and estuaries, where fishing, crabbing, and tide-pooling make all that commercialism seem irrelevant, if not irreverent. One curious thing Lincoln City has done to attract tourism is to seed its beaches with home-blown glass floats—2,000 every year, created by regional craftsmen. So they didn't make the haphazard voyage all the way from Japan—they're still pretty, and

A brilliant rainbow blesses Pacific City, at the southern end of the Three Capes loop. Though the Oregon coast can receive over 80 inches of rain a year, most of it falls from November to March.

the hunt can amuse children for hours. Another new tradition, Lincoln City's summer and fall kite-flying festivals bring in visitors by the thousands to watch the ocean air fill with color.

North of Lincoln City U.S. 101 swerves inland toward the Coast Range to avoid a series of three capes. So much the better for those who want to get off the main highway and see some of the most spectacular shoreline on the West Coast. Narrow roads loop past dairy farms, spruce forests, and small villages; spurs off these roads lead to heart-pounding clifftops where pelicans dive beyond a crashing surf, and wave-chiseled rocks stand as monuments to endurance. At the south end, Cape Kiwanda is a tremendous sandstone bluff. To actually stand on the cape, one has to get out and take a short beach walk to the top of a dune. Early mornings, fishermen tow small flat-bottomed boats out from the beach parking lot into the surf. This fleet of dories then motors out through slamming, deck-swabbing waves; in the late afternoon the fishermen come pounding back in, running their dories up on the sand as close to their trailers as possible. A small crowd often gathers to watch this ritual, and to buy fresh tuna and salmon right off the boat. Dories used to ply the Nestucca River, but when gill netting was banned there in the 1920s the river fishermen took to the sea. When the dories are out, there's still plenty of activity on Kiwanda—hang-glider pilots and surfers take full advantage of the cape's dunes and winds.

❋

NEXT UP, windswept appendix-shaped Cape Lookout is perhaps at its moody best on a cloudy day. An easy one-hour trail winds through a lush rain forest of mossy Sitka spruce, western hemlock, and red cedar towering over salmonberry and shrubby salal. The trail noses along the cape's edge in places for ocean views to the south, nearly as fine as those from the 500-foot-high cliff at the end of the cape. Between Cape Lookout and Cape Meares, the scenic detour to U.S. 101 dips through the little town of Netarts, situated at the mouth of Netarts Bay. Long-legged wading birds pose in the bay's shallows, and harbor seals sometimes haul out on the sandbars. One has to pull off the road to enter the resort village of Oceanside, just north. But the small effort is repaid by a view of a triad of arched rocks standing a few hundred yards out—constant wave action has whittled openings in the bases, where the water slams through with a powerful spray. Sea birds congregate on the tops of the rocks, while sea lions take to the lower ledges.

Crisp and ready for action, the Tillamook Bay Coast Guard Station in Garibaldi averages more than 250 search-and-rescue cases a year in the Three Capes area.

But the most exhilarating views on the Three Capes Scenic Route are from Cape Meares. From the high bluffs one sees rocks jutting like black teeth in a wave-whipped sea, while flecks of foam come rising up the cliffs like clouds of white feathers. The wind buffets this shore, a pewter sky blending down to a nipped sea. On raw days or clear, the place is a stunner—for Portlanders, 80 miles east, the first real gulp of sea air. A short trail leads to a natural wonder called the Octopus Tree, a massive multi-trunked Sitka spruce perched near cliff's edge. Each of its trunk limbs measure at least six feet around. Deer browse the underbrush nearby, in a virgin forest some 200 years old.

Another trail wanders along the cliff to views of Three Arch Rocks south, as well as closer rocks, teeming with murres, pigeon guillemots, and pelagic cormorants. From here they sound like a swarm of mosquitoes. Train binoculars on a rock and thousands of little domestic scenes come into focus—birds squabbling over nesting space, adults winging back and forth from sea to rock top, chicks taking the plunge and gliding to the water far below. Every year hundreds of thousands of murres nest on these rocks. The murres seek fish as far away as the mouth of the Columbia River, more than 50 miles north. They dive deep, staying submerged for up to four minutes

Crossing a lilac Columbia River, the 4.1--mile Astoria-Megler Bridge links Oregon with Washington.

in their search for tomcod, anchovy, smelt, and squid. These seabirds make such a thrilling sight it's hard to believe that tourists in the early 1900s found pleasure boating around the rocks and shooting at nesting birds. The pointless slaughter finally galvanized public action in the form of protective laws.

As if the grand cliffs and seabirds weren't enough, Cape Meares also holds an 1890 lighthouse. Imagine living on this isolated point a hundred years ago, when sailors at sea depended on you for their lives. You had to trim the wicks, fill and light the kerosene or oil-vapor lamp, and, if a malfunction occurred, hand turn the big first-order Fresnel lens all night until you could make repairs in the light of day. You and your family and the assistant keeper's family were the only people for miles around. Once every few weeks you'd row up bay to Tillamook for food you couldn't grow in your garden. That's also where the nearest doctor lived, and if you had to go in the middle of the night it was a lengthy, harrowing buggy ride. But the important thing was that 20 miles out at sea on a stormy night, a captain could see your light and know where he was.

With electricity in 1934, much of the keeper's busywork was gone, and by 1963 so was the keeper, the light replaced by an automated beacon. Still, of Oregon's nine coastal lights, six still aid in navigation, including Cape Meares, which primarily serves area fishermen. And the tower still stands as a reminder of the pioneering spirit, a beacon of hope perched on the edge of the continent. If any place along the Oregon coast deserves a caption with the following lines from Byron, certainly it is here: "There is a rapture on the lonely shore, there is society, where none intrudes, by the deep sea, and music in its roar."

THOUGH NOT ON THE COAST, the town of Tillamook sits squarely on the Pacific Coast Highway, just off the Three Capes drive. In other words, it's unavoidable, which is not a bad thing. The air of Tillamook is wholesomely redolent of cows. That's because the green pastures of Tillamook County are home to 28,000 dairy cows, whose milk is converted annually into 55 million pounds of cheese. The Tillamook County Creamery Association is where the alchemy happens, and visitors may wander about, view the high-tech operation through picture windows, see informational videos, and

As in a classic Japanese painting, a lonely conifer clings to a bluff in Oregon's Samuel H. Boardman Scenic Corridor. Here the coastal mountains slant right to the edge of 200-foot oceanside bluffs.

Reenactors raise the Stars and Stripes at Fort Stevens, built during the Civil War to protect the entrance to the Columbia River. The property is now a state park.

Coasting in Fort Stevens State Park, a biker passes the century-old wreck of the *Peter Iredale*, a
reminder that the waters around the Columbia River bar are the "Graveyard of the Pacific."

Snug and dry, members of the Lewis and Clark team work by candlelight in a reenactment at Fort Clatsop, a reconstruction of the winter 1805-06 campsite.

check out displays on the hundred-plus-year history of local cheesemaking—the sailboat on the company logo refers to the days when butter and cheese were transported only by sea. Best of all, though, are the samples of various cheeses. Of course, the main point of this hospitality is the tour-bus-friendly gift, cheese, and ice cream shops. The smart money comes away with at least a hunk of cheese and a cone of rich Tillamook ice cream.

Just to the north, the vacation town of Cannon Beach has strict ordinances that prevent unattractive sprawl. They cannot prevent hordes of beachgoers from descending upon the town in summer and fall. But who can blame people for flocking to this artsy hamlet and its awe-inspiring beaches? Galleries, shops, restaurants, and cars jam Hemlock Street, while out on the long sandy beach stands one of Oregon's most-photographed icons. Haystack Rock, one of the tallest rocks on the Pacific coast, rises 235 feet; it stands close enough in for waders to explore its tide pools at low tide, and far enough out to strand those not paying attention to high tide.

Haystack is also visible from the headlands of Ecola State Park, a 1,300-acre parcel of verdant old-growth forest and rocky coastline. Members of the Lewis and Clark expedition hiked along here searching for whale blubber to supplement their meager diet in the winter of 1805-06. Clark was not happy about climbing through the dense forest to the 1,000-foot-high cliffs of Tillamook Head. Ever fond of superlatives, he wrote, "the Steepest worst & highest mountain I ever assended." Yet when he had made it to the top and had a great view of the ocean, he reported, "I beheld the grandest and most pleasing prospect which my eyes ever surveyed." They found a beached whale on Cannon Beach, but it had been mostly picked over by the local Tillamook Indians.

IN THE NORTHWEST CORNER of the state, Fort Clatsop commemorates the winter campsite of Lewis and Clark. The explorers spent a miserable winter here, waterlogged, flea-bitten, hungry, and bored. They suffered from colds, rheumatism, and venereal disease. The only silver lining was that they had made it all the way across the continent to the Pacific coast, an unprecedented scientific and military expedition. And as soon as the weather eased up they were going home. The re-created fort, set in a grove of tall spruce, is an amazingly authentic time machine to that end-of-the-trail encampment—costumed interpreters stroll about, water pings into rain barrels (especially in winter), the fort smells of wood smoke and elk hides, and at the canoe launch hand-hewn dugouts look ready to go.

Clustered on the mouth of the mighty Columbia, the town of Astoria came into being not long after Lewis and Clark had left the area, making it the oldest American settlement west of the Rocky Mountains. An 1811 fur-trading post led to a thriving port for fishing and logging by mid-century. In the late 1800s it was salmon that fueled the local economy—so many millions of salmon migrated upriver that it appeared as though you could walk across the river on their backs. Some 40 canneries operated on Astoria's waterfront; when the salmon began to diminish, the canneries packaged tuna. Now the town has not a single cannery. But commercial fishing and port activities keep Astoria humming. Tourism does play a big role here, but the town hangs on to its workingman's roots, with its comfortable taverns, low-fashion downtown stores, and an excellent maritime museum.

The best overview of Astoria and its situation on the river is from the Astoria Column, a 125-foot monument on a high residential hill. The historical marker was dedicated in 1926, and restored in 1995 at a cost of one million dollars—about 37 times the amount it cost in the first place. But this is no average small-town marker.

Spiraling all the way up the column is a bas-relief frieze depicting key moments in local history from Clatsop Indians and Lewis and Clark to fur traders and the transcontinental railroad. A gift shop here sells balsa gliders to launch from the column's observation deck. But the magnificent view suffices—the town shrinks to insignificance in this wide perspective of the Columbia flowing into the sea. The view also helps one appreciate just how tough it must have been to link Oregon to Washington. The 4.1-mile Astoria-Megler Bridge over the Columbia is proof that it was done. Up until 1966, the only way to get to Washington other than by water was to drive 55 miles upriver and take the 1930 Longview Bridge. But on August 27, 1966, the new bridge opened to great fanfare, with 30,000 people in attendance.

Winter storms can roar into the mouth of the Columbia with winds up to 150 miles per hour, packing waves up to 30 feet and making this one of the most hazardous river bars in the world. The "Graveyard of the Pacific" has claimed more than 700 lives in 2,000 shipwrecks. With waves piling in against one of the country's largest rivers by volume, little wonder that William Clark described it as an "agitated gut swelling, boiling and whirling in every direction." The 20 members of Astoria's Columbia River Bar Pilots are experts at negotiating the treacherous currents and shoals around the bar. Assisting ships through the mouth of the river, they are licensed to pilot anything from a 100-foot tug to a 1,100-foot tanker. Even with their dauntless skill, they close the river bar to shipping up to ten times a year during the worst storms. Such is their respect for the infamous Columbia River bar.

The northwesternmost point of Oregon, Clatsop Spit defines the lower lip of the mouth of the Columbia. A coastal fort here guarded the river's entrance from the Civil War to World War II. The only action came on June 21, 1942, when a Japanese submarine fired on the fort but did no damage. Now a state park occupies the spit. On one of its beaches, the skeletal remains of a four-masted bark protrude from the surf; the ship wrecked here in 1906 with no loss of life.

A viewing platform on the end of the spit gives huge sweeping vistas of the ocean, beach, and flat-forested area all around. I climbed up for a look at the corner of Oregon, wind making my eyes water. A ship was heading into the river's broad mouth; the ocean was chopped up and clouds were scudding. It was a satisfyingly tremendous view, with a wide deserted beach to the south and, four miles away, high headlands across the river in Washington. ✳

Barking and bellowing, wild Steller sea lions congregate on a rock at the Sea Lion Caves north of Florence. The herd occupies the 1,500-foot-long cavern in autumn and winter.

islands and rain forests

WASHINGTON

✵

THERE IS NO RULE that the coast has to have an ocean view. The fractured edge of Washington State, indented by Canada's Vancouver Island, includes estuaries, islands, straits, and bays. Unlike the cliff-and-cove uniformity of Oregon's coast, the Washington shoreline presents an ever varying spectacle. Pacific waves batter low tidelands in the south, while up on the Olympic Peninsula smooth-stone beaches and a temperate rain forest spread beneath a lordly range of snow-capped peaks. The many islands of Puget Sound, with their little communities and anchorages, further complicate the picture. One common thread is rain. Rain wracks this coast in winter and spring. Yet while one side of the Olympic Peninsula bears the brunt of colossal storms that can produce waves two stories high, the other side goes practically dry. The mountains create a rain-shadow effect by blocking that soaked ocean air. Up to 150 inches of rain can fall annually along the Pacific coast, while locations east of the mountains might receive as little as 16.

Another common theme is hardiness. The Indians and settlers who first lived on this wind-and-rain-battered jigsaw coast had to learn to love the soaking green forests and fog-bound shores. Those who could not moved inland, or farther away. Modern travelers who have journeyed up the coast from points south will find this a far cry from the sunny shores of Southern California. Just when you think you have the Pacific coast figured out, a final twist adds an unexpected dimension.

Towering above the Experience Music Project in Seattle Center, the 605-foot-tall Space Needle has been the Northwest's iconic structure since the 1962 World's Fair.

Down in the southwest corner of the state, the Lewis and Clark expedition reached its goal in November of 1805. Clark recorded that his "men appear much Satisfied with their trip beholding with estonishment the high waves dashing against the rocks & this emence Ocian." They spent the next ten days exploring Cape Disappointment (named earlier by an English sea captain frustrated trying to find the mouth of the Columbia River), then decided to winter on the opposite shore of the Columbia.

On a recent trip here I stopped by the excellent Lewis and Clark Interpretive Center. After a look at the exhibits, I took a short hike through a coastal forest to the Cape Disappointment Lighthouse. From this windy headland one can sense the thrill of those early explorers beholding the wide Columbia slipping into an even wider Pacific. Down below, seabirds shoot the tips of the swells. Astoria, Oregon, is a distant smudge way across the river, and the undeveloped shore of Fort Stevens State Park arcs southward. The 1856 lighthouse is the oldest operating light on the West Coast, but its beam has not been enough to prevent some 2,000 wrecks at the treacherous mouth of the Columbia. From up high, though, the view is serene and compelling. Posted in front of the lighthouse, Tennyson's "Crossing the Bar" feels just right here: "Sunset and evening star, And one clear call for me! And may there be no moaning of the bar, When I put out to sea. . . ."

Like Fort Stevens across in Oregon, Fort Canby protected the mouth of the river from the Civil War to World War II. Today Fort Canby is part of Cape Disappointment State Park, which spreads over the southern tip of the Long Beach Peninsula. Though the fort is a distant memory, the U.S. Coast Guard station here is the largest search-and-rescue outfit on the Pacific coast. In addition to rescuing endangered mariners within 50 nautical miles, the station provides maritime law enforcement and is also home to the National Motor Lifeboat School.

THE 28-MILE SLIVER OF BEACH, grassy dunes, and bayside wetlands known as the Long Beach Peninsula was a bountiful table of endless oysters for the Chinook Indians. Today the oysters, mostly farmed, are still plentiful. At the south end, the vacation communities of Seaview and Long Beach stay busy in summer catering to fishermen and beachgoers. Off-season there can be practically empty stretches of shops and motels. A good place to go in any season is the 1896 Shelburne Inn, a snug Victorian-style hostelry with a pub and restaurant and elegant breakfasts served family style.

Among the possibilities are Willapa Bay fresh oyster quiche with homemade biscuits, and baked French toast with mixed berries and nuts topped with champagne cranberry-orange glaze. At that groaning table, I met a party of plant-loving British travelers, who were finishing up the Lewis and Clark trail. They were keeping a tally of all the plants they had seen—more than 200 in a fortnight. Afterwards I took a walk through the neighborhood of old-fashioned beach cottages and out onto a nearly deserted beach, with lump-in-the-throat views of an expansive sea.

I found that not all the locals were happy with the Lewis and Clark trail, and the attendant bicentennial hoopla. A salty middle-aged redhead, as skinny as her greyhound, told me, "I hate that thing. Long Beach stole valuable beachfront property from Seaview just so they could put in a concrete walking trail. And Lewis and Clark weren't even there. It was under 20 feet of water then. As an artist, I told the property owners to put up wooden fences on both sides of the trail and I'll paint Lewis and Clark in scuba gear." She lived on a cranberry farm, "a buffer of 150 acres," but even so felt the pinch of Californians and others moving in to rural Washington for its peace and quiet.

Sandwiched between the ocean and bay sides, the peninsula's thin middle supports several cranberry farms. Many of the cranberries grown here and in Grayland, farther up the Pacific coast, end up in Ocean Spray drinks. Bandon and Seaside,

Fishing floats hang outside Jessie's Ilwaco Fish Company. Situated to the northeast of Cape Disappointment, Ilwaco was named for local Chinook resident Elowahka Jim.

The 1856 Cape Disappointment Lighthouse shines at twilight. Capt. John Meares named the cape
in 1788 after his failed attempts to locate the mouth of the Columbia River.

Morning dew highlights spider webs in a tidal marsh near Westport. Grays Harbor, spreading northward from here, ranks as one of the largest estuaries north of San Francisco.

Daylight dies on a rocky sentinel on remote Rialto Beach north of La Push, in Olympic National Park.

Native American Theresa Parker makes twine the old way, by hand—and mouth—at the Makah Cultural and Research Center in Neah Bay.

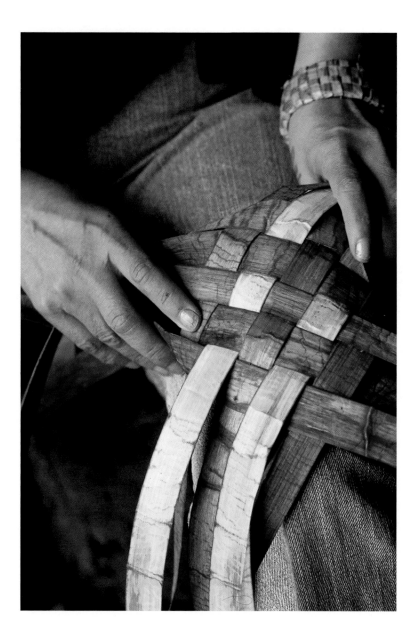

Weaving baskets from western red cedar bark, Theresa Parker helps preserve ancient
tradition at the Makah Indian Reservation on Cape Flattery.

Readying a vessel for sea, a member of the Port Townsend Shipwrights Co-op fills boat seams with batting. The co-op has been restoring and building boats since its founding in 1981.

Oregon, also grow cranberries, as do communities in Massachusetts, New Jersey, and Wisconsin. The Pacific Coast Cranberry Research Foundation in the middle of the Long Beach Peninsula operates a demonstration farm that gives consumers a peek into the business. The berries grow on vines in sandy or peaty soil; sprinklers turn on automatically if the temperature gets too cold or too hot, thus protecting the fruit from frost and heat. During the June blooming, farms rent hives of pollinating honey bees—up to four hives per acre. They also place raptor perches around the area to encourage hawks and owls to police the fields for rodents.

The Long Beach Peninsula anchors the lower end and western edges of Willapa Bay, the second largest estuary (after San Francisco Bay) on the Pacific coast. In this gentle mingling of fresh- and salt water, a host of wildlife thrives. Great blue herons hunt crustaceans on the mudflats; chum, coho, and chinook salmon migrate up the streams to spawn; Roosevelt elk graze the meadows and take cover in remnant old-growth forests; beaver and river otter nose along the watery margins for fish and other prey. From the dunes to the salt marshes and forests, species as divergent as great brown pelicans and black bears make a good living in this largely unpeopled area. The Willapa National Wildlife Refuge protects about 15,000 acres of this rich and varied habitat, and provides a stopover for tens of thousands of migratory birds.

Willapa Bay lies along the western edge of Pacific County, about half of which is owned by Weyerhauser. Trees are still big business in this area. The highway courses through the patchwork forest—some sections filled in, others a clear-cut expanse of stumps and debris. Roadside signs boast the speed of a parcel's regrowth. Western hemlocks that sprouted as volunteer seedlings 40 to 50 years ago are already mature and ready for harvesting. Every year Weyerhauser plants millions of seedlings. At the Pacific County Historical Society Museum in South Bend, I learned that most areas are now on their third harvest, with much greater yields than the original old-growth forest. Still, with computers and lasers doing more of the work that used to require expert hands and eyes, employment in the mills has dropped in recent years.

The road up around the top of Willapa Bay gives sweeping views of the bay and the tip of Long Beach Peninsula, then passes through beachy communities like Grayland, with trailers and small lots decorated with toy windmills, wooden seagulls, and Styrofoam floats. A sign out one window advertises the Pot Shed nursery, while out the other stands Fantasy Cabins, whose themed accommodations include Jardin D'Amour and Shipwreck at Taboo Lagoon. The road swings on around to the next furrow in the coast, Grays Harbor. In 2000 Willapa Bay and Grays Harbor together produced more than half of all the state's oysters: Each year they harvest about 149 million oysters, or 32 million dollars' worth. Willapa's harvest alone accounts for 15 percent of the national total.

*

AT THE SOUTHERN END of Grays Harbor, Westhaven State Park is situated on a wide and wild beach. The area is so flat that you need to climb a dune to get a view, but then you can see for miles in every direction—out to sea, up to the harbor, and back to the forested mainland. The beach is popular for surfing, walking, fishing, and whale-watching. A surfer told me he uses the riptide to take him out along the jetty, because the waves are simply too strong to paddle past. As for the water temperature, "I've been colder surfing in Hawaii without a wetsuit than with one here. It's just a little restrictive. The problem today was with the current. Every day it's a different current, a different wave."

Back around to the east where the Chehalis River slides into Grays Harbor, the logging town of Aberdeen has a look of faded glory. Fine Victorian houses still adorn its hilly streets; pool halls and taverns have moved into some of the stalwart

Misty sunrise on a primeval woodland: In the low-elevation forests of Olympic National Park, a canopy of western hemlock, red cedar, and Douglas fir grows up to 200 feet high.

downtown buildings—a throwback to the old days of gambling dens and honky-tonks—and the old movie palace stands vacant. A pulp mill is still prominent on the river east of town, and the steady stream of traffic indicates the continued march of commerce, if not outright prosperity. With more automation, slimmer forest pickings, and a ban on logging in federal- and state-owned old-growth forest, the economy has shifted around toward courting tourists.

Just west of town, Grays Harbor National Wildlife Refuge hosts hundreds of thousands of migrating birds. The nature trail out to the tidal mudflats is unusual in that it starts out beside a landing strip. Bowerman Airfield is not exactly crowded with takeoffs and landings, so the main noise is generally wind. Marsh wrens, yellowthroats, and yellow warblers nest in the willow thickets, and in the flats beyond herons stand on stilt legs at low tide and shorebirds flock at high tide. The peak of

shorebird activity is in spring, when the basin here becomes a key staging area on the northward journey.

The North Beach area of Grays Harbor extends for more than 25 miles along the coast, from Damon Point all the way to the Quinault River in the Quinault Indian Reservation. Near the southern tip, Ocean Shores was laid out as a resort community in the 1960s. Wide streets of a contained business area are lined with beachware shops, restaurants, and other concerns, while to the south neat yards spread in front of modest homes. There is a feeling of ampleness, as if the planners wanted everyone to have lots of room.

The beach itself is wide and six miles long, and you can drive on it as long as you stay above the clam beds. "Just don't leave your car out as the tide is coming in," a tourism bureau official told me. "Do you want the number of our tow truck operator just in case?" she teased. I drove out onto the beach and immediately felt my tires spinning in soft sand. But I soon found the wide avenue of hard pack and drove a few miles from one entrance to another. Huge flocks of juvenile gulls stood about, barely bothering to get out of the way. On summer weekends hundreds of cars line the shore. A section of beach closed to traffic offers people a chance to stroll the surf in peace.

About halfway up Washington's Pacific shore, the great Olympic Peninsula begins. The wide sandy beaches of the south give way to cliffs and sea stacks, reminiscent of Oregon's coast. Most of this northern coast is part of Olympic National Park, a vast treasury of rugged coast, rain forest, and jagged peaks. The park's 63-mile Pacific shoreline is one of the longest stretches of undeveloped coast in the contiguous United States. The lower ten miles, up to Ruby Beach, are easy enough to get to. But then the highway veers inland, and only a couple of small roads weave their way out to the remote sections of the coast. What lies out there is an untamed borderland, where bears forage in tide pools and bald eagles swoop from giant nests. Rain in mythic proportions animates the water and sky and forest like a god. And in summer shrouds of fog lift to reveal totemic wonders—whales, seabirds, elk—that vanish as suddenly as they appear.

Along these cobbled and sandy beaches, wave-thrown driftwood as much as 120 feet long and 6 feet in diameter lies tossed like pickup sticks. Giant sea stacks and sea arches are slowly sculpted by waves that perpetually shatter against them. Just offshore, hundreds of little islands host puffins, auklets, gulls, murres, cormorants, and other seabirds, as well as seals and sea lions. Protecting the shoreline and coastal waters, the Olympic Coast National Marine Sanctuary embraces 3,310 square miles—more than twice the size of the national park—effectively extending the park well out to sea. Within the sanctuary, forests of kelp extending 70 feet up from the sea floor provide havens for fish and sponges, while gulls and sea otters rest in the floating beds of the kelp forest "canopy." Farther out on reefs and in undersea canyons live a teeming variety of wondrous creatures, including fish-eating anemones, 100-year-old rockfish, and the world's largest octopi.

A few miles inland lies a West Coast wonder. Watered by 12 feet of rain a year, a temperate rain forest grows in rank profusion on the western side of the Olympic Peninsula. Coastal fog can add another 30 inches of moisture. The result is an emerald city of Sitka spruce, Douglas fir, western red cedar, club moss, sword fern, and lichens. Record-size old-growth trees, some topping 200 feet, flourish in this fairy-tale world of dripping shadows and arrowed sunlight. Fallen trees become nurse logs for seedlings; the growing never stops. Unlike the sweltering jungles of the tropics, a temperate rain forest is cooler and fresher, varying in temperature from about 32 to

70 degrees. These rare ecosystems are found in southern Chile, New Zealand, and here in the Pacific Northwest. Not only is this the wettest place in the contiguous states, the moss-cushioned forest floor makes it one of the quietest. Other than the occasional airplane drone, few man-made noises penetrate the dense cocoon of the Hoh Rain Forest. The quietest times, of course, are intervals between the drumming of rain. After all, this is an area where good weather means it's not currently pouring.

At higher elevations, lowland and subalpine forests grow, thinning as they ascend the heights. Up here meadows of wildflowers rim glacial lakes, and severe weather stunts growth—three-foot-tall trees may be a century old. On the roof of the park rise mountains topping 7,000 feet, aloof in their snow-clad Olympian splendor. The park's highest peak, 7,969-foot Mount Olympus can receive over 50 feet of snow in a year, thanks to the tremendous amount of moisture piling in from the Pacific. Glaciers and melting snow gouge the rocky slopes with infinite patience, carrying bits of the mountain down to the sea.

One of the highlights of the park's mountainous region, Hurricane Ridge Road makes a winding ascent of Hurricane Ridge, climbing nearly 5,200 feet in 17 miles. At the top spread magnificent views of the Olympics, the Strait of Juan de Fuca, and Vancouver Island. Even in the fall, as I discovered on one trip, ice and snow can close portions of the road, and conditions can change hourly. I was able to drive 12 miles up, at which point I got out and walked another mile or so to where the road was covered in snow. Deer tracks disappeared along the flanks of the mountain, and beyond lay ridge after snow-crowned ridge.

ON THE NORTHWEST CORNER of the Olympic Peninsula, Cape Flattery lies at the lonely end of a road that snakes far beyond the park boundaries and across the Makah Indian Reservation. From here there are terrific views of the Pacific, the Strait of Juan de Fuca, and wild wave-bashed inlets. A fascinating museum holds the remnants of an ancient Makah village buried in a mudslide 500 years ago and excavated in the 1970s by a team from Washington State University. The Makah, "the people who live by the rocks and seagulls," have lived here for more than 4,000 years. Their totem poles still grace the small cemetery and marina. In 1788 they first saw "the house on the water people," American explorers in a ship captained by Robert Gray.

Whaling was a traditional part of Makah culture until the 1920s, when they

From Queen Anne Hill, the Space Needle and Seattle skyline sparkle in evening light. Seattle Center hosts the Northwest Folklife Festival (right), an annual extravaganza of dancing, crafts, and demonstrations showcasing folk art from more than 100 countries.

voluntarily gave it up. They stirred up a controversy among animal-rights activists when they announced plans in the late 1990s to resume hunting whales, as their treaty affirmed their existing right to do. Though their experienced whalers had long since died, the Makah managed in the spring of 1999 to kill a whale, using a motor-boat and rifles to supplement the traditional cedar canoe and harpoons. For many environmentalists it was an end to the myth of the Indian as guardian spirit of the natural world. The Makah claim the hunt was prepared for as traditionally as possi-ble, and the whale products were shared at a feeding of three shifts of diners in the local gym. To the Makah, the hunt was for food and cultural activities, and promoted tribal unity; opponents believe the hunters intended to sell the meat abroad.

Small cottages and farms line the highway east of the Olympic gateway town of Port Angeles. Relatively little rain falls out here in the shadow of the Olympics. One of the most interesting places on the north side of Olympic Peninsula, Dungeness National Wildlife Refuge occupies a 5.5-mile-long spit of sand and gravel beach. Curving out into the Strait of Juan de Fuca, the refuge provides a much-needed (Continued on page 173)

In the golden afternoon, kite flyers revel at Seattle's Lake Union, once a vital link between
Puget Sound and Lake Washington.

Saved from demolition in 1971, Pike Place Market has been a Seattle tradition ever since,
with fresh seafood stalls among the most popular attractions.

Containers stand ready for unloading at the Port of Seattle, fifth largest container port in the United States. In addition to its trade operations, the port handles more than 150 annual cruise-ship calls.

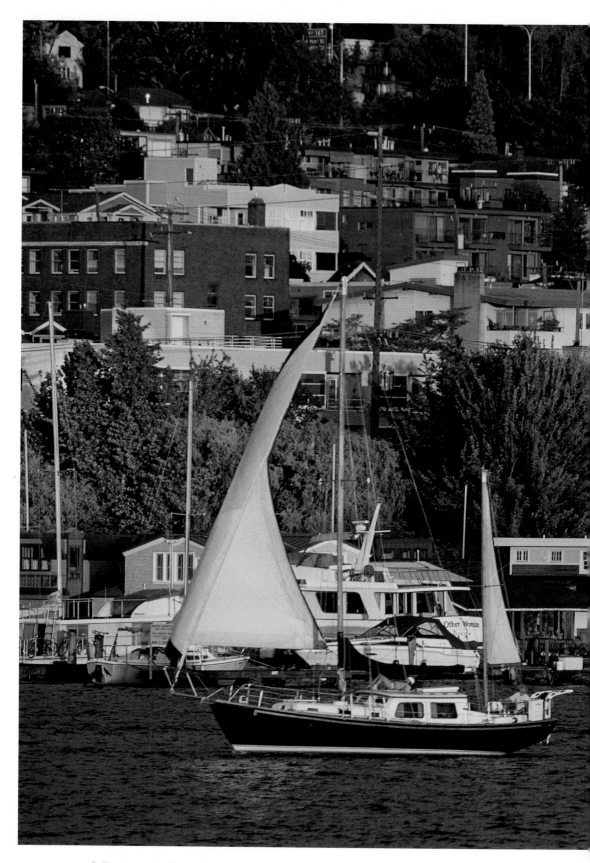

Sailboats provide the scenics for dwellers of condominiums crowding the hillsides above
Lake Union; marinas, restaurants, and houseboats line the shore.

(Continued from page 164)

sanctuary for harbor seals, Pacific black brant (a small goose), and 250 other sea- and shorebirds. At sunset from here the San Juan Islands appear to float on a layer of velvet.

Perched on the northeast corner of the Olympic Peninsula, Port Townsend is one of the most delightful little towns on the West Coast. The well-built seaport thrived on fishing and lumber in the late 1800s, becoming second only to New York in the number of ships calling in. Expecting the arrival of the transcontinental railroad, the town underwent a building boom in the late 1880s. But the railroad went to Seattle instead, and Port Townsend's fortunes went south. Decades of economic decline stunted the town's further growth. About the only thing built in the 1920s was a pulp and paper mill, still a major employer. What remained when restoration efforts began in the 1950s was a small, time-warped seaport filled with Victorian architectural treasures. By the end of the century Port Townsend had been reborn as a handsome maritime village, ideal for yachters and weekend visitors. In addition to browsing the friendly shops and museums, people come for the many arts events and to participate in workshops on sailmaking, ropemaking, boat repair, and other marine trades.

Port Townsend's main commercial district lies along Water Street, while many fine houses with turrets, pergolas, and fancy trimwork stand on a bluff above. From several places there are wonderful views of Puget Sound and, on clear days, the Olympic and Cascade ranges. Small-scale old hotels and B&Bs in Victorian homes dot the town. I stayed at the Palace Hotel, a rambling old structure with stained glass, high ceilings, and arched windows. According to the proprietors it had served as a railroad office, saloon, and brothel—known then as the "Palace of Sweets." In a similar vein, an entire exhibit in the historical museum focuses on bordellos. Clearly the town likes to play up its rollicking past, perhaps with the idea that the sheen of age transforms the bawdy into the romantic.

One of the most romantic movies of the 1980s was filmed in part at nearby Fort Worden State Park. Built in the late 1890s to help protect the area against sea invasion, the former bastion is now a serene park with views across sparkling Puget Sound. The grounds and buildings served as a backdrop for *An Officer and a Gentleman*. Officer's Row is a smart line-up of wood-frame piles with colonnaded porches; they are now available for rent as vacation homes. At the end of the row, the elegant 12-room Commanding Officer's Quarters serves duty as a house museum. To the north stands a small marine science center, with touch tanks and aquariums. Elsewhere on the grounds

An artist at the Pilchuck Glass School north of Seattle examines his creation. Prominent glass artist Dale Chihuly and his patrons founded the school in 1971.

Whale watchers get a glimpse of an orca surfacing in Puget Sound. Cruise boats here also encounter Dall porpoises, seals, bald eagles, sea birds, and the occasional sea lion and minke whale.

of this swords-to-plowshares park, concerts and festivals take place regularly.

A few miles south of Port Townsend, the Northwest School of Wooden Boat-building has for 23 years taught students how to make seaworthy vessels. As many as 44 students attend the boat-building vocational program, and another 300 or so attend summer workshops, handcrafting up to eight vessels at a time. The facilities include two 8,000-square-foot buildings with a sail loft, milling shop, classrooms, and boat shops, busy with the sound of power sewing machines, wood-turning lathes, planers, shapers, and band saws. The smell of freshly milled wood mingles with the brine of the bay to imbue a satisfying maritime flavor.

It's about five miles by ferry across the sound from Port Townsend to Whid-bey Island. The other option is to drive around through Seattle and take the bridge across Deception Pass—a total of over 200 miles. In other words, ferries are often the best, and sometimes only, way to island hop in Puget Sound. Commercial ferries have been operating in these waters since the mid 1880s, when Hudson's Bay Company steamers were put into service. Now state owned, a 29-ferry fleet shuttles passengers between 20 ports in Washington and British Columbia. On nice weekends, waits can be long, but the ferry ride is an outing in itself—an inexpensive way to get out on the water and see birds and perhaps marine mammals.

At 55 miles in length, Whidbey is the largest island in the Puget Sound region. Farmlands and forest surround the few small towns, and cliffy coves and rocky beaches dollop the outline. Up at the island's northern end, a narrow channel joins the Strait of Juan de Fuca with Skagit Bay. English Capt. George Vancouver sailed the area in 1792, naming the island after one of his officers, Joseph Whidbey. At first Vancouver was fooled, thinking the island was a peninsula. Realizing that what he thought was an inlet was actually a throughway, he named it Deception Pass. Washington's most popular state park, Deception Pass State Park, occupies the island's northern nub, where high bluffs and the soaring Deception Pass Bridge give spectacular views of the narrow pass and the many islands peppering the waters. Pedestrians can cross the towering steel span for an adrenaline rush, especially if the tide is shooting in or out between Rosario Strait and Skagit Bay. Back in the park, the calls of loons and thrushes echo on the lakes, and minks and muskrats slink through the marshes.

Just south of Whidbey Island stands the nerve center of northwest Washington—Seattle. The geographical setting alone is unequalled by any American city. On a recent airplane flight, I could see it all—the city skyscrapers, the waterways and islands, the sawtooth Olympics on one horizon, and popping splendidly above a cloudbank, the presiding spirit of Seattle, 14,411-foot-high Mt. Rainier, its muscled flanks gleaming white and pink in the late afternoon light.

With such an uplifting geography, a mild climate, and a position on the Pacific rim, it's little wonder that Seattle has prospered in recent decades like few other cities. Artistic and culinary trends originate here with remarkable frequency. And consider the number of Seattle-based businesses that are now household names—Starbucks, REI, Eddie Bauer, Nintendo, Nordstrom, Amazon.com, Boeing, Microsoft, and others. What with airplanes, software, lumber, and discount retailing, Seattle's economy has a nicely diversified portfolio.

Promoters note that rainfall totals are actually less here than in, for instance, New York. They don't mention the number of days it rains—a lot. But the frequent showers freshen the air and keep the parks a vivid green. And whenever the weather breaks, people head out—jogging, biking, kayaking. *Men's Fitness* magazine rated this the country's second fittest city in 2003.

Named for friendly Suquamish chief Sealth, Seattle was first settled in 1851. When the Northern Pacific Railroad picked Tacoma as its western terminus, Seattle appeared destined to play second fiddle. But the town kept growing, *(Continued on page 180)*

An equestrian farm on Orcas Island offers something different from the expected roster of kayaking, bicycling, hiking, and other favorite island activities.

Feathering glassy water, a ferry approaches Friday Harbor at San Juan Island. One of the country's largest ferry systems, Washington's 29 ferries transport some 25 million passengers a year.

Sunset is prime whale-watching time at San Juan Island's 1917 Lime Kiln Lighthouse.

rebuilding after a disastrous fire in 1889. Iron, concrete, and stone replaced much of the city's wood, yet lumber was what kept pouring out, fueling the town's economy. Then, with the Klondike gold rush of the late 1890s, Seattle became the major outfitter, and a muddy little waterfront burg began changing into a shipping and marketing behemoth. The Seattle World's Fair in 1962 marked the beginning of the modern era in the Pacific Northwest. Emerging from the spotlight, Seattle showed that it could attract a wide variety of businesses, and prove equally attractive to visitors and prospective residents.

Leftover from that world's fair, the Seattle Center northwest of downtown remains one of the city's greatest magnets. The Monorail and Space Needle, still icons of Seattle, have an enduring look of newness, even now in their retro space-age modernism. The 607-foot tower, topped by a saucer-shaped revolving restaurant and observation room, offers splendid views of the city skyline, the Olympics, and the Cascades. And the sleek Monorail still whooshes passengers back and forth from downtown. Other Seattle Center institutions likewise appear poised for several more decades of use—a continually updated hands-on science center, a children's museum, sculpture garden, sports arena, and opera house. The new kid on the block, the Experience Music Project is a salute to American popular music in a showy building designed by Frank Gehry. The structure's jazzy curves, colors, and glass suggest "fun zone" more than "interactive museum," as if the architect wanted you to enter an emotional state rather than a place. Pulsing music videos and participatory exhibits dazzle forever-young visitors and herald the future as much as anything at Seattle Center.

Downtown, locals and outsiders alike flock to Pike Place Market, in many ways the heart of Seattle. Unlike the typical sanitized, polished-wood market found in many big cities, sprawling Pike Place has an earthy nonchalance, confident of its heritage. The farmer's market that started here in 1907 was nearly torn down during an urban renewal drive in the 1960s. Local citizens rallied to save the dozen derelict old buildings; the result was a new nine-acre national historic district. One can now wander this bustling emporium of fresh produce, flowers, and seafood, dazed by the intermingled smells and sounds. The temptation to buy is overwhelming—with the waterfront just below, those gleaming piles of salmon, geoduck clams, and Dungeness crab look too fresh to pass up. You can practically taste the sea. Many of the vendors ship all over the world. And for those buyers who don't want to bother with ice, there's always smoked fish.

The market's multilevel main arcade has gift shops, galleries, and eateries down below, and vendors above. At Pike Place Fish, mongers not only energetically hawk their seafood, they throw fish from one seller to another—a crowd-pleasing spectacle. I watched for a long time—the sight of big fish flying through the air has a compelling simplicity. After lunch at a brew pub and shopping for family gifts, I went across the street to the original Starbucks. This is where the polished wood floors are. As well as good rich coffee. The Seattle coffee culture, exported far and wide, had its origins in this little shop in 1971. There's nothing much remarkable about this Starbucks compared to any other; that reliable sameness in some 8,000 shops around the world is part of the chain's success story.

※

OUT ON THE WATERFRONT, one can see the pumping of Seattle's main artery. Huge factory trawlers maneuver to the north piers; ferries and cruise ships depart for the San Juans and beyond; waterbirds dart past looking for easy pickings; tourists haunt the waterside pubs and cafés. The renovated Bell Street Pier, with its informative maritime discovery center, is one of the best places for watching the action.

I caught up with an old friend, Joe Hunter, who until recently was a vice president of a Seattle fishing company heavily invested in Russian fisheries; at one time they were the largest producer of king crab in the world. After the company sold off most of its holdings to Russian partners, Joe teamed up with a local architect to found a design/building firm. "The story of the fishing industry here," he said, "is the decline and near collapse of the industry. Just in the last two years, yachts have been allowed to dock at Fishermen's Terminal for the first time, because there haven't been enough commercial fishing vessels to fill the berths. The problem isn't resource collapse—most commercially significant species are doing fine. The problem is price collapse. Many fishermen can't make a living anymore, and the worldwide growth in aquaculture is the single biggest nail in the coffin. For a time it was like a gold rush, it was very exciting. But it's not an industry that makes a lot of sense in terms of efficiency."

The Belltown neighborhood behind the pier is a bohemian enclave of old apartment buildings, secondhand stores, and music clubs that fostered grunge and other styles. Real-estate values have risen here with the recent influx of solid citizenry. Another interesting neighborhood lies east of downtown on Capitol Hill. Named for the capitol that was never built (Olympia got that honor), this leafy district has a jumble of lifestyles. On shady streets, millionaires inhabit early 20th-century mansions, while Broadway draws an eclectic crowd—gay, painted, pierced. Almost everybody is young, yet there are few children. I did manage to find one toy store amid the incense shops, bars, and restaurants.

An oyster farmer on Orcas Island tends his crop. Oysters grown in Orcas Island's Crescent Bay have a firmer texture than those grown on San Juan Island.

Blossom-time in Moran State Park: Foggy days bring focus to things near at hand on this Orcas Island sanctuary, whose highlands afford splendid views when the curtain lifts.

Spreading smiles all around, Orcas Island sculptor Joan Rora Baugh turns a tremendous piece of driftwood into art. In addition to totemic figures, whales and bears make popular driftwood subjects.

Capitol Hill's green space is the delightful Volunteer Park. Along with the Olmsted-designed fountains, flower beds, and promenades, there are robust views from atop the old brick water tower. Unlike at the Space Needle, this view is free, and unadulterated by a gift shop. From here you can take in the city and its neighborhoods, Puget Sound, and Lake Washington. And you can even see the Space Needle. But the park's real gem is the Seattle Asian Art Museum. Among many priceless treasures is a Chinese collection dating to the Neolithic period. I also liked the Japanese tea garden, where you can eat sandwiches to the accompaniment of flutes and trickling water. In a city with a population that's 13 percent Asian (the largest minority), this museum is a reminder of the ties between the Pacific coast and its neighbor to the west.

To get a closer look at some waterside activity, I drove out to the Ballard Locks (officially, the Hiram M. Chittenden Locks). Pleasure craft were locking through the canal that connects Puget Sound with Lake Washington. I learned that some 75,000 vessels use these locks every year—mostly recreational boats, but also fishing boats, research boats, sightseeing boats, container ships, log rafts, and barges loaded with sand, gravel, and fuel. The eight-mile-long canal opened in 1917 after six years of construction. On the other side of the canal, a fish ladder helps salmon and steelhead migrate upstream. I looked through the viewing window, though unfortunately saw no fish. But I went away convinced that the U.S. Army Corps of Engineers is doing what it can for the declining population of wild salmon.

The inner workings of even bigger technology are on display in Everett, not far north. The port town first vaulted into the big time with an economic boom in 1900. But the really big time came in the 1960s when Boeing picked a spot near a small commercial airfield and former air force base south of town as the site for its jumbo-jet factory. On tours of the mind-bogglingly large facilities, visitors can see workers assembling 747s, 767s, and 777s. The main factory building covers some 98 acres.

☀

WHERE DOES THE NATION'S Pacific coast end? Cape Flattery? The mainland border with Canada? Alaska? Any terminal point seems arbitrary, so why don't we conclude with the San Juan Islands, that 700-plus-island-and-reef archipelago sprinkled across the straits separating Washington and Vancouver Island. Like stepping stones from one country to another, Canada's Gulf Islands belong to this constellation, separated only by an invisible boundary line.

That boundary was in hot dispute in 1859. The Oregon Treaty of 1846 held that the dividing line extended "to the middle of the channel which separates the continent from Vancouver's Island." And therein lay the rub. A look at the map shows there is not just one channel but two (at least). If you drew a line exactly between the continent and Vancouver Island, some islands would be split in half. But clearly San Juan would go on the Canadian side. The Americans on San Juan thought the line should go in the Haro Strait, west of the island—San Juan, in other words, would be American. The British jointly occupying the island disagreed. In 1859 an American farmer shot and killed a straying British pig. When the British tried to arrest him, a company of U.S. infantry was sent to his aid. The British responded with three warships, but with orders to avoid an armed clash if possible. The American leader, Capt. George Pickett, though hugely outnumbered, refused to back down. Four years later at Gettysburg, Pickett would learn a hard lesson about opposing a superior force, but this time he was successful. After two months of tense standoff, the President had to send Army commander Gen. Winfield Scott to keep war from breaking out. Scott worked out a joint military occupation—Americans on one end of the island,

British on the other—that lasted for 12 years. A new treaty finally gave the island to the United States.

San Juan is now the most populous of the islands, with nearly 7,000 residents. Summer visitors swell that figure, but even so there are plenty of wild and pastoral delights. Most people choose to avoid the hassle of bringing their cars, relying instead on a shuttle-bus service or bikes to get around the island. Hiking trails through San Juan Island National Historical Park and other places give inspiring views of the Cascade and Olympic Mountains, British Columbia, and many islands—some not more than a rock with a few trees. On secluded beaches, terns and gulls gather, while the lagoons are good places to watch great blue herons and bald eagles.

Of the three other islands serviced by ferry—Orcas, Lopez, and Shaw—Orcas Island has the most to offer visitors. The largest of the islands at 57 square miles, Orcas has a handful of pleasant little waterside villages, where moored sailboats bob and small inns are decorated with local crafts. Moran State Park holds 2,407-foot Mount Constitution, highest point in the islands and probably the best perch (other than an airplane) for viewing the layout of the archipelago and the surrounding majestic mountains. Orcas Island was named for a Spanish viceroy, but there are also orcas, or killer whales, inhabiting the waters of the San Juans. Three pods, totaling about 85 animals, live here, along with minke whales. The largest members of the dolphin family, orcas travel and hunt in groups, going after salmon, seals, and smaller dolphins. When they surface, the telltale spout gives way to the black blade of a fin. Sometimes the orca will leap entirely clear of the water, grab a gulp of air, and dive back in. The reentry is much less splashy and more graceful than that of other whales.

Whale-watching boats scurry about the San Juan Islands from May to September. Many people prefer the peace and quiet of a sea kayak, in which any encounter with wildlife seems more of a fortuitous gift. In either event, the thrill of seeing an orca or a dolphin or a bald eagle is never to be forgotten. It becomes a story to take home and bring to mind whenever you need an escape from the pressures of life.

The possibility for such encounters motivates many a trip along the Pacific coast. A trip just to see a whale—what a ridiculously simple idea. Yet we will always be drawn seaward, if only for that glimmer of meaning that comes in a close look at a creature other than ourselves, a creature whose mysteries lie deeper than we can ever fathom. ❉

Trolling for handouts, a gull follows a Puget Sound ferry in the rosy glow of late afternoon. A standard mode of transportation in the Seattle area, ferries see a sharp rise in business during the summer.

ABOUT THE AUTHOR

JOHN M. THOMPSON has written seven National Geographic Books, including *The Revolutionary War* and *Wildlands of the Upper South*. He is at work now on two books: *American Journeys* and *Almanac of American History*. His usual beat being the Southeast, he particularly enjoyed researching and writing about the vastly different personality of The Western Edge.

ABOUT THE PHOTOGRAPHER

As a freelance photographer for the National Geographic Society since 1985, PHIL SCHERMEISTER has crisscrossed North America working on such projects as the Tarahumara Indians of Mexico, the Pony Express Trail, and the Cherokee Indian Trail of Tears. Assignments for the Society's Book Division have taken him to many of our nation's national parks, forests, and monuments. He recently completed an article on Yosemite National Park for the January 2005 issue of NATIONAL GEOGRAPHIC magazine. He and his wife, Laureen, and their two children live in the Sierra Nevada foothills town of Sonora, California.

ACKNOWLEDGMENTS

The author would like to acknowledge the following people for their help with this book: Joan Tapper, Steve Siegel, Ian Bosserman, Maria Mudd Ruth, Joe Hunter, Mckee Poland, Sarah French, and Margo Browning.

ADDITIONAL READING

The reader may wish to consult the *National Geographic Index* for related articles and books.

The following titles may also be of interest:

Coastal California, by John Doerper. Fodor's Compass American Guides, 2000
Two Years Before the Mast, by Richard Henry Dana. Buccaneer Books, 1984
Snow Falling on Cedars, by David Guterson. Vintage Books, 1995

INDEX

america's western edge

By John M. Thompson
Photographs by Phil Schermeister

Published by the National Geographic Society

John M. Fahey, Jr., *President and Chief Executive Officer*
Gilbert M. Grosvenor, *Chairman of the Board*
Nina D. Hoffman, *Executive Vice President*

Prepared by the Book Division

Kevin Mulroy, *Vice President and Editor-in-Chief*
Charles Kogod, *Illustrations Director*
Marianne R. Koszorus, *Design Director*
Barbara Brownell Grogan, *Executive Editor*

Staff for this Book

Rebecca Lescaze, *Project and Text Editor*
Jane Menyawi, *Illustrations Editor*
Cinda Rose, *Art Director*
Victoria G. Jones, *Researcher*
Carl Mehler, *Director of Maps*
Sven M. Dolling, *Map Research*
Greg Ugiansky, *Map Production*
R. Gary Colbert, *Production Director*
Lewis Bassford, *Production Project Manager*
Meredith Wilcox, *Illustrations Assistant*
Robert Swanson, *Indexer*

Manufacturing and Quality Control

Christopher A. Liedel, *Chief Financial Officer*
Phillip L. Schlosser, *Managing Director*
John T. Dunn, *Technical Director*
Alan Kerr, *Manager*

One of the world's largest nonprofit scientific and educational organizations, the National Geographic Society was founded in 1888 "for the increase and diffusion of geographic knowledge." Fulfilling this mission, the Society educates and inspires millions every day through its magazines, books, television programs, videos, maps and atlases, research grants, the National Geographic Bee, teacher workshops, and innovative classroom materials. The Society is supported through membership dues, charitable gifts, and income from the sale of its educational products. This support is vital to National Geographic's mission to increase global understanding and promote conservation of our planet through exploration, research, and education. For more information, please call 1-800-NGS LINE (647-5463) or write to the following address:

NATIONAL GEOGRAPHIC SOCIETY
1145 17th Street N.W.
Washington, D.C. 20036-4688 U.S.A.
Visit the Society's Web site at
www.nationalgeographic.com.

Library of Congress Cataloging-in-Publication Data

Thompson, John (John Milliken), 1959-
    America's western edge / by John Thompson ;
photographs by Phil Schermeister.
        p. cm.
    Includes index.
    ISBN 0 7922-3811-7 — ISBN 0-7922-3812-5
(deluxe ed.)
    1. Pacific Coast (U.S.)—Description and travel. 2.
Pacific Coast (U.S.)—pictorial works. I. Schermeister,
Phil. II. Title.
    F851.T48 2005
    917.9—dc22

                                    2004064986